Mental Models

50 Thinking Tools That Distinguish Successful People From All Others in the Crowd; Judgment, Analysis, and Learning. Have a Clear Mindset to Allow for Positive Change

Peter H. king

Table of Contents

Chapter 1: Decision-Making for Speed and Context

How fast should we make our decisions? It is not easy to balance efforts geared towards gathering information to make a choice and the losses you can incur because you took your time to make a decision. Some situations keep on increasing with complexity; the more you delay, the more the benefit disappears. For instance, people with the duty of responding to emergencies suffer the loss of life every minute they delay to take action. With our current changing environment, speed is required in making decisions to generate value. In the above situation, complexity only slows the speed for making the decisions, and this may worsen situations. There are so many factors to consider when making decisions in organizations; budget, data from different sources, performance analytics, and much more. A good leader knows that the faster he or she makes the best decision, the faster he or she can implement it. Given a chance, you should refine your decision-making process, but you may need some false starts to get the process.

While there is no quick fix, there are some mental models that leaders can adopt to help them speed up the decision-making process. A mental model is enlightenment on a person's process of thought on how things work in reality. It represents the world, the relationship between a person's view on his or her actions and its various procedures and their repercussions. They can change behavior and show us how to work out problems and handling tasks. All models are different, and none of them is best suited for all of us, so it is important to find out what best suits your needs. Let us look at mental models that enable us to make decisions in the shortest time possible and at the same time, make correct decisions. They are:

Address "Important" Ignore "Urgent"

Most of us make plans for the following day before we go to bed. Unfortunately, only a few accomplish everything they had laid out for the next day. Do you know why? We lose our focus on urgent and trivial tasks like meetings, emails, calls, or catch-ups. How can you make out what is important and what is urgent in your life?

Urgent tasks are tasks that require your immediate attention. They have deadlines, and you have to give them your attention immediately. They are tasks like emails, calls, or meetings. On the other hand, important tasks are tasks that help us achieve our long-term goals. Unfortunately, important tasks get overshadowed by urgent tasks. Now, it is important to plan our days in such a way that despite your limited time, you manage to set aside time for these important tasks. Let us look at the Eisenhower decision matrix that can assist us in planning our days in the manner mentioned above.

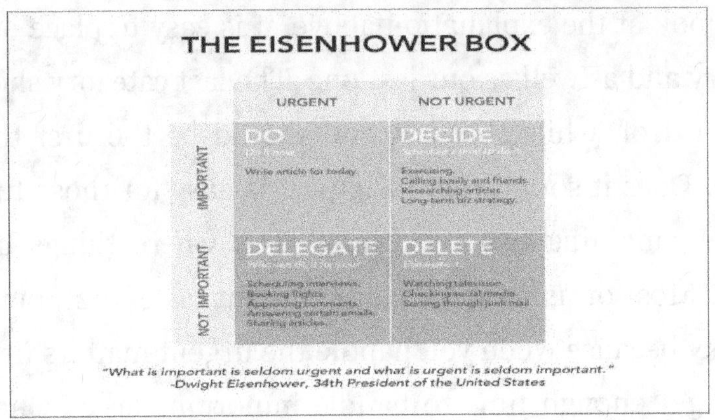

A man of many titles developed the above diagram; United States Army general, World War II Supreme Commander, and US President for two terms Dwight Eisenhower. He divided it into four categories, as explained below:

I. Important and Urgent (top left corner)- In this category, you can put stuff like problems, crises, or deadlines.

II. Important and Not Urgent (top right corner) – In our second category, we can have things like recreation, relationships, or long-term goals.

III. Not important and Urgent (Bottom left corner) – Our third category should consist of day to day interruptions such as meetings, calls, or emails.

IV. Not Important and Not Urgent (Bottom right corner) – Our last category, which is easy to eliminate, may consist of things like pleasant tasks or time wasters.

If you look at the explanation above, it is easy to place our first category and as well as our last one. The last category should be gotten rid of, while the first one should be the first thing to handle. Does it sound easy? Right, it is easy for those two, but for the remaining two quadrants, it is where things become murky. Most of us tend to handle urgent tasks first, but it can be tricky because when you handle the urgent matters first, you do not get enough time to handle important tasks. One thing you should be aware of is that the world has a surplus of urgent tasks, and they will always be in excess. How many times have you had an important matter to handle, but you lack the time? Well, that is the point whereby you alternate urgent and important matters. You should always try and create time and only postpone what you would be comfortable leaving undone if you died. How can you create urgency in important tasks?

The best way to make important tasks urgent is by giving them a deadline. Deadlines make all matters urgent, and you are obliged to handle them immediately. When tasks lack deadlines, they lose their importance tag after all; you still have time to take care of them. In most cases, important tasks are huge, and to set deadlines, you have to divide them into smaller tasks and give them deadlines. How do you set these deadlines? You can use David Allen's approach to Getting Things Done. The first thing you need to know is the next action that will give your project momentum and set a serious deadline for it. Make sure that you don't just set deadlines but let them be non-negotiable. In case you do not meet the deadlines, there will be serious consequences. Let's look at an example; if you miss paying your rent, your landlord will pressure you with calls until you pay. In case you still miss paying, you will have a case to answer in court, and you may be evicted. Did you notice how serious the consequences are? When you set deadlines for important tasks, it is not automation of urgency, and at the same time, there are no serious consequences in case you miss the deadline. I know you can set a deadline easily, but let me show you a few ways that you can use to make it more significant.

a) Make it public

State your deadline publicly to give it a degree of seriousness. When you do that, you will not only be accountable for yourself alone but to other people as well. You will have the pressure to hit your deadline because there will be so many people to explain to when you fail to hit it.

b) Carrot and stick

Our second great way to make our deadlines serious is by having a carrot when you hit the deadline and a stick when you miss it. Simply put, a carrot is a reward for completing your project on time, and a stick is a punishment you get for missing the deadline. So, you are wondering, it is easy to reward myself, but how can I punish myself? For instance, you can give your friend a check of $1000 to give to your worst political organization in case you don't hit the deadline.

c) Make others accountable

How should you treat other people involved in your project with whom you are working together to accomplish your long-term goal? They should also know the importance you've given to the important deadlines. State it in black and white that there will be no room for missed deadlines. You should also commit yourself to check in on their progress, and if you find someone lagging behind the deadline, you should not shy away from having a serious talk on it. If you are not strict on following up on the deadlines, they will not know how important deadlines are to you, and in most cases, you will find them pushing some deadlines back and missing some.

d) Set personal reminders

When you have reminders now and then, it will not be easy to ignore your deadlines. You have to do whatever it takes to have constant reminders around you, such as sticky notes around your office or calendar timers.

Urgent tasks will always be in excess, but you should create time and direct all your energy in handling important tasks because when you miss them, you will regret later in life.

Visualize All the Dominoes

Visualizing all dominos enables a person to make well-informed decisions. When making decisions, most of us think of one domino, the immediate impact that will be caused if we make the decision. As human beings, we are wired to look at decisions as isolate and without consequences, which is known as the first-order thinking. In this thinking, we only think of the decision to be made at that point and don't consider how making that decision will affect the future. It is also known as the first dominos-thinking. When we make this decision, the results may affect other people as well, unpredictable or otherwise. To avoid such consequences, we should visualize all the dominos, otherwise known as the second dominos-thinking. In this model, you project the future and weigh down all the probable results and conduct a cost-benefit analysis for your decision. Second, dominos thinking helps you to gather more information and to think twice before making the decision. You get a view of all dominos and check what will happen if the first domino is tipped and look at all the long-term consequences of your decision.

Howard Marks gave a good example of how this may play well in life. In 1936, John Keynes wrote a hypothetical newspaper contest where readers would be given 100 photos and required to choose the six prettiest girls and a reward to those who chose the girls with the most votes. Remember, the contest was on the prettiest girls and not on the most popular girls. To win in this competition, it is important to know who the average readers would consider as a pretty girl. At the same time, you should also consider that each entrant had his perspective on pretty, and this brings another order to the strategy. This strategy can be moved from one level of thinking to another, and in each one, you should predict the result and at the same time, consider the decisions of other entrants. When you think of the other entrant's decision, you are already in the third domino, and some go further to other dominos depending on the complexity of the situation. Most of the time, things happen, followed by a chain of events. You should not base your decision on the gratification only, but you should look past and view all the things that could go wrong if you made that decision. Train yourself to view each decision as having several dominos. It might be tedious, but its effects are lifelong.

Second-order thinking helps you to look at a decision through many scenarios making you make more informed decisions. Why is it not easy to implement second-order thinking? Because we are not wired to do so as human beings, but the good thing is that we can learn to. Second-order helps you to think clearly and allows you to rise above average. When you use second-order thinking, you predict the future well and see things more clearly than those you compete with. When you adopt this model, you improve your decisions. Let us look at some guiding questions that Howard Marks gave us to help in second-order thinking.

- How large will the future be affected by the current decision made? Look at the effects beyond your immediate concerns and check if the decisions will achieve their purpose.

- Which are the consequences of your decision? Think of more results other than the primary one. Think of the effect on other people and think of the consequences of the success or failure of your decision.

- What is the probability of succeeding? Look at your decision objectively and weigh its success or failure. Conduct a cost-benefit ratio analysis of your decision.

- What will other people think? You could ask a few people on their thoughts if you made a certain decision. You should also be careful not to be swept off your feet by unpopular opinion.

- How different is my thinking from everyone else? Look at what is different in your decision than popular knowledge and check for anything that you could be missing.

- Are other people visualizing the fall of more dominos? Seek to find the viewpoint of other people on the fall of dominos but be keen because not all information given will be valid, but you can source for more information.

By visualizing all the dominos, you are exposing all the results to make an informed decision.

Make Reversible Decisions

Most of us think that having a lot of research on something translates to the best decision. Sometimes it happens, but in other cases, it is not the case. Successful people use the simplest techniques to avoid wasting time on deliberations on issues. Some famous people have such simple techniques from Steve Jobs' default settings of saying no to calculations to Elon Musk's first principle. Our third mental model is by Jeff Bezos, founder of Amazon.com.

Bezos wonders if a decision is reversible or irreversible. When a decision is reversible, it is easy to make it without taking time and without all the information needed. On the other hand, if it is an irreversible decision, we take time and make sure that we have all the information needed before we conclude on it. Bezos was employed before he founded Amazon.com, and he reasoned that if his creation failed, he would be absorbed back to employment. He used his model to make that decision. If he started his company and it failed, he reasoned out that it would still be a lesson learned, and he would not have any regrets for it. Since his decision was reversible, he had a plan B up his sleeve of going back to employment. Luckily, the model worked for his favor, and he is still reaping the benefits to date.

How to decide in uncertain circumstances

For instance, if you decide to open a warehouse because of the positive reviews you read online, you are not certain that people will lease space in your warehouse or if they won't. Despite that, you still use the part information you got from the review to make a decision, being aware that it's okay if customers do not lease storage space in your warehouse. Some situations have riskier uncertainties. For instance, when you decide to take a new job, you have no idea about the company culture or how you will relate with the other employees. Reversible decisions do not consume our time as we can make them with partial information. If they do not work, we can take it as a lesson and learn from it. Most of the time, these decisions would only worsen things if you took the time and energy to get 100% information on them.

Reversible decisions should not be an excuse to make poor decisions. Rather, it is believed that the decisions made should match the time and energy utilized on them. When you are in a position to make decisions quickly, you attain an added advantage. Small companies on their initial stages of formation are advantaged because they move with velocity. Contrary, the established companies move with speed. What is the difference between the two? When a company moves with velocity, it is moving at high speed towards its goals, whereas if the company is moving with speed, it means that the company is growing but not necessarily towards achieving its goals. Our model, therefore, explains why small companies at their initial stages are at an advantage when they make quick decisions.

When you make a decision, you get data that you use to shape the future. Therefore, the faster you make decisions, the better for the company. Our model should be in every decision that you make in the company as it will enable you to recognize poor decisions and to pivot instead of sticking to choices of the past because of the belief of sunk costs. Likewise, it is important to enable you to make mistakes as lessons and acquired information that will help you to make decisions in the future. Bezos explained in this model that reversible decisions are like doors that offer passage to both directions, while irreversible directions only offer one direction passage such that you cannot come out when you get in. Most of our decisions are reversible even though we waste time and resources if they fail, but at the same time, we get a life lesson. Bezos explained that the irreversible decisions should be made carefully and with great deliberation because if you enter that door, there is no turn back. He called these decisions Type 1 decisions. Fortunately, most decisions are reversible, and he called them Type 2 decisions where the repercussions are not long-lived. If the decision made is not appropriate, there is an opportunity to walk through the door again. Type 1 decisions are famous for companies at their start-up stage while type 2 decisions are famous with large organizations where decision making is slow and involves no sufficient experiments and therefore reduces invention. Bezo's model shows us the route to fight the inclination on type 2 decisions. He teaches us what has assisted him in building and retaining the start-up tempo in building his company. Organizations should work towards being effective and not following the laid down rules. Every corporate should learn the advantage of reversible decisions and make them move at a quick pace, just like the start-up c.

Stay Within the action

Our fifth model is one that will help today's leaders to make decisions with the fear of either getting embarrassed or hurting other people. One famous comedian cemented the purpose of this model by stating that his rule dictates that he should decide on anything that gains 70% approval because it increases to 80% when you remove the other options from the table, and you diminish the pain of making a decision. Colin Powel, the former US Secretary, formed this mental model that helps us to make decisions within the shortest time possible. He states that to make a decision, one should have a minimum of 40% and a maximum of 70 % of the needed information. In this range, you are in a position to make a good decision and a fast one than most people. Powell felt that if you have 40% of the information, it would not be enough to make a decision, and the results would be full of mistakes. He also pointed out that by deciding that point would be putting a lot at risk while aiming for speed. Decisions made below 40% of the required information may result in:

- Correct decisions that don't address the situation fully because of lacking some aspects.
- Ill-informed decisions from some biased people.
- Wrong decisions that seemed good but were made in haste.
- The wrong decision could have been avoided if you seek more information.

On the other hand, when you seek for more than 70% of the information, it will only slow you down and overwhelm you. At the same time, that opportunity may be snatched by someone else who might start later than you or at the same time as you had started. You will be putting all at risk in the search for certainty. It can also result in:

- Loss of clients because of impatience.
- Employees may be forced to do some damage control as they wait for a decision to be made.
- You may lose revenue because of a decrease in sales.
- Implications as a result of delaying to remove some things from the shelf.

Foolproof plans do not exist, and by seeking them, you will only over-analyze your situation and at the same time, keep postponing your decision. In the range between 40% and 70%, there lies all the information you may need, and the little bit left can be filled with your intuition. This mental model can be used in all walks of life, and we can replace our 40%-70% information with just about anything; courage, learned, planned, read, confidence, etc. At 40%, you have all the information to make the first step ad with the idea that you will gather more as you play out the decision. When you make a decision in the shortest time possible, you only experience few or no downsides. This model helps you to decide on less information and also generalizing. You get the ability to ignore all the grey areas and at the same time, make rational justifications when you are making your decision. It helps you to pay attention to only the general information and its effect on you. Powell's rule separates successful leaders from the average ones. Great leaders use their intuition to make difficult decisions, whereas most of us never listen to our guts. Most of us seek certainty and 100% surety that the decision we are making is the right one, which is impossible. People who seek 100% surety on the information they seek they tend to fit in being employed rather than employing others. Now, shortly when a tough decision will face you, apply Powell's rule by getting enough information to make a good decision, and then the remaining part relies on your gut.

Minimize Regret 0%

Our sixth model is a lesson from Jeff Bezos. He had an idea, but he had not decided on it yet. His idea was to begin an online store for selling books. The good thing is that he talked openly about it and even informed his boss, who advised him to mull over his thoughts before he made decisions. Bezos thought for 48 hours, but he needed a mental model that would enable him to make the right decision. He needed to look at the world and what is important for him. Luckily, for him, he came across the Regret Minimization Framework, and just like magic, it worked for him. It is a simple model, but it helped him to make that important decision. Regret minimization model aims at finding out if you will regret not doing something after several years.

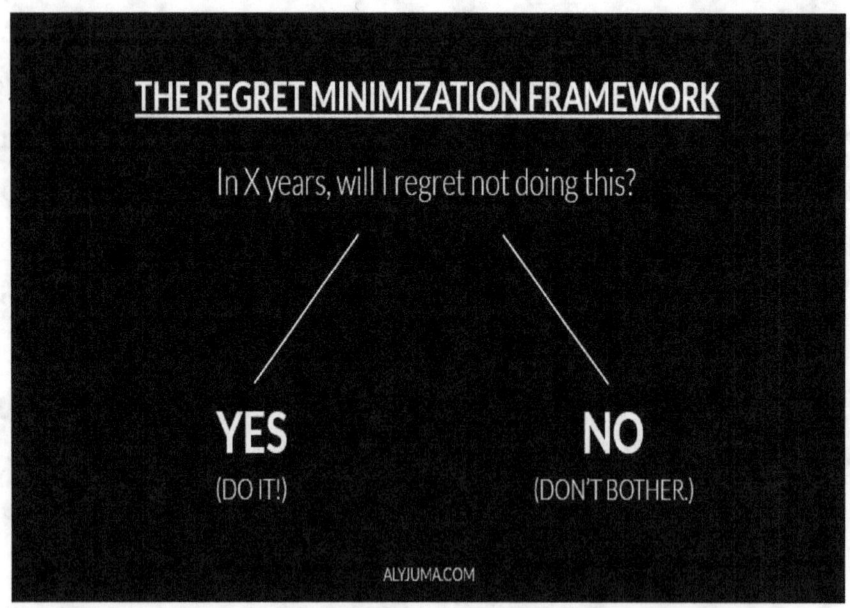

The idea behind this model is to place yourself in the future and view your decisions from that point. Bezos placed himself at 80 years and asked himself if he would regret not starting the online books store. He got a clear answer, and he explained that the model helped him understand that at 80 years, he would not regret trying to start the company, trying the new thing known as the internet, but he was sure that he would regret not trying to implement his idea. Regret Minimization Framework pushes you beyond the present and past all the current doubts and fears. It gives you an open view of the future to scrutinize things from that angle. When you move to the future, you view your decision in a new light, a light that absorbs all your doubts and fears into the scheme. RMF is a life model that you can use any time you encounter a difficult decision. It is a powerful tool to use to influence your uncertainties.

Bezos went for his idea, and with where his company is positioned globally, he made it. Consequent research supports him in one feature of his decision, just as Bezos assumed. Science tells us that most of us tend to regret unattempted actions more than we regret the failure of our decisions. In this model, Bezos is not advocating that you should jump into every risky venture that you come across. Rather, he considers that his RMF should assist all of us to weigh our personal goals and values to make a good decision. If you can look at yourself at 80 years and think of how your thoughts will be at that time, it helps you to reduce some current confusion. In case you are having a hard time deciding your life, it is never late to try.

Chapter 2: How to See More Clearly

Have you ever thought of the detailed use of binoculars in your life? Binoculars give us focus on things that are far and that are foreign to us. You can watch as a bird build a nest and feed its little ones, you can watch as a lion hunts its prey, or you can watch the alignment of our solar system. All these uses and many more, but, unfortunately, a binocular blinds us from the things that are below our noses. When you choose to use binoculars, you can only have the far view and miss the finer details below your nose. To binoculars, it is impossible to see both ways, but in life, it may be difficult but not impossible. You have to train your brain to stop jumping to conclusions and filling in the blank spaces. You may be attentive, but it is not possible to rely on what you hear or see to make a full picture of what is on the ground. It becomes difficult because you might rely on information from a biased person, or your beliefs and biases may lead you to make a faulty judgment. Our inbuilt wires do not allow us to see or think objectively, and it becomes easier to prevent it when we acknowledge that.

This chapter allows you to view the world as what it is, something that most of us struggle with. The mental models in this chapter will help you to see through false realities and distractions of our lives and enable you to get to the truth as close as you can. They are tools that will assist you more than you can imagine. For instance, we've all heard of the saying that to make an informed decision on a location that you won't locate to, it would be important if you visited it all the four seasons. You can also visit the place in the two worst seasons before making an informed decision. If you visit the place for a few days, it would be unwise to make a decision basing on that. All objects or situations are subject to change because of different conditions and events. When it comes to gathering information, there is no shortcut. You should get as much information as possible before making a decision. The process might be tedious and overwhelming but very vital for better knowledge and intelligence collection. Having this mindset encourages you to a lot of information on any situation or topic from different environments, backgrounds, and conditions as you can. When you have a lot of information at your disposal, you avoid making blind assumptions, inaccurate projections, and snap judgments. To have a broader overview of all situations, let us look at specific templates of mental models.

Ignore "Black Swans"

This model helps you to understand how you should not allow your thinking to be influenced by outliers. Did you know that Europe at large believed that the swan was only in white up until the 18th century? They reasoned that they have never seen a swan of any other color, and with that absence, they had no reason to believe that there was a swan of any other color. In 1697, it marked the beginning of changing that belief. Willem

De Vlamingh, a Dutch explorer, traveled to Australia. During his exploration, he strolled along the Swan River, and together with his team, they saw what was new to any European's eyes. They saw lots of black swans swimming in the river. This new sight made a strong impact, and they rewrote some tenets in Zoology on the belief that all swans were white. Imagine if swans were as many in colors as the colors on the rainbow.

Statistician Nassim Nicholas used the above history to come up with the black swan theory. He takes the black swan as the unpredictable events in our lives that cause great change in our understanding and perceptions. Yet, to Nassim, the black swan should not change our perceptions or beliefs because it is a strange outliner. The black swan should create awareness, but it should not be accounted for every day. Seeing another color of the swan should have been translated that black swans exist in both black and white color but should not result in throwing out the whole belief system of zoology. For instance, if you learn that a tree was struck by lightning in your neighborhood, you may get frightened, and you may take a further step to install some lightning rods. Now, should that same event change your lifestyle? Should you stay indoors throughout after that to avoid being struck by lightning? Does it mean that you should change towns to avoid lightning, or should you move underground and start living like a mole?

According to Taleb, the thinkers before him only took care of the improbabilities. He explained that the unexpected might be foretold by getting information from statistics calculated on the past observations. Taleb said that the usual happenings did not concern him, but if you want to understand a situation, you should look at it from the abnormal point of view. Is it possible to have an understanding of health with no knowledge of epidemics? Well, normal is irrelevant, and if you look at your social life, you will notice the jumps and shocks in it, but in reality, all we know about it is normal. It happens because the bell curve does not pay attention to the large deviations, but at the same time, it makes us think that it has covered all the uncertainties.

Look for Equilibrium Points

There are so many ways we can explain them equilibrium points mental model, but the easiest is the Boombustology, where a small ball lies on a curved shape, as shown below.

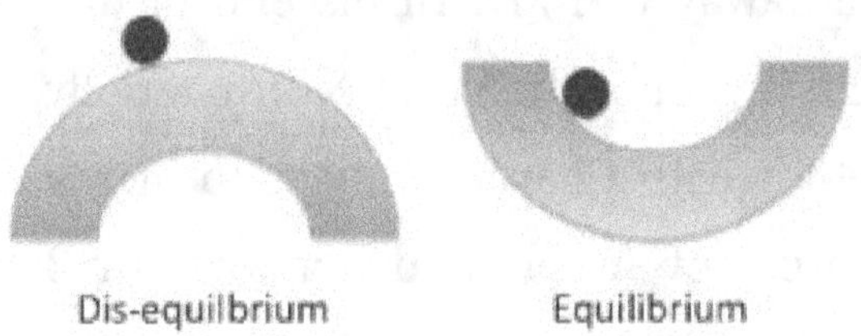

In the two diagrams below, equilibrium can only be achieved if we leave them alone and allow the ball to find its location. In disequilibrium, the ball does not find a location to settle. Newton uses three laws to describe this model. He used planets to demonstrate how gravity behaves between two objects. He explained that the sun's gravity is offset by the planet's velocity, therefore, equating the powers and creating equilibrium. What is the equilibrium? It is the balance between opposing forces. There different types of equilibrium. Static equilibrium is when the system is resting while dynamic equilibrium is where there is a presence of two or more forces, and they have equal powers.

Hagstrom Robert shows us the difference between these two equilibriums in the Last Liberal Arts. He explains that when a scale has equal weights on both sides, it represents static equilibrium whereas our bodies represent dynamic equilibrium; when our bodies lose heat to maintain the balance with the sugar consumptions

Supply and Demand + Equilibrium

Warren Buffet purchased 11.2 million ounces of silver through Berkshire Hathaway in 1997. In his end of the year letter, he stated that the inventory had reduced materially, and they had decided together with Charlie Munger to increase the price to equate the forces of supply and demand. In Boombustology, Mansharamani explains that the most approach towards equilibrium is the notion that increased prices produce new supply that reduces the prices. It is also believed that reduced prices result in new demand that, in turn, hikes the prices. Forces of supply and demand enable us to make informed decisions. For instance, investing in aluminum is a poor investment because you can only make good returns if the supply is tight. If there is excess in the market, the prices reduce, and consequently, you do not make sustainable profits. In such a scenario, only low-cost producers make profits because they will still maintain full production, and the cycle keeps repeating itself. Opportunities to make returns only come around when the demand is more than the production because of the increase in demand and the decrease in supply. In finance, Mansharamani explains that it is made up of two components; the reality trend and the misconception. He expounds further using real estates. He explains that, in reality, people are willing to lend and pay for the increased prices. This trend has a misconception relating to it that real estate prices are not connected to the willingness to lend. Moreover, when the financial institutions are open to lending, the buyers increase, making the financial institutions to feel secure and give more loans.

Feedback Loops and Equilibrium

William Lidwell & co. explained the law of equilibrium in Universal Principles of Design. He explains that feedback is created when reactions circles back to make an effect on themselves. In reality, all systems have a feedback loop; machines, animals, business, to name a few. We have two feedback loops. The positive feedback increases production, which in turn causes decline or growth. Contrary, negative feedback reduces production and maintains the system at an equilibrium point. Positive feedback brings change and negative repercussions if the negative loop does not regulate them. For instance, in the 1950s, plastic helmets with padding replaced the leather ones because of the increase in neck injuries. The helmets added protection, but players till took great risks when playing, resulting in more neck injuries than before. When designers concentrated on the player's behaviors, they created a positive loop, which made the players use their head and neck vigorously, and therefore, designers created more plastic helmets that were harder and padded more. Negative feedback loops are change resisters. For example, Segway Human uses negative feedback to maintain equilibrium. When riders lean forward, it accelerates, and when the rider leans backward, it decelerates to place the system in equilibrium. To make this change effectively, they work towards making changes every minute.

Wait for the Regression to the Mean

Regression to the mean helps us to reduce judgment and focus on our weak spots in our way of thinking. Sir Francis Galton was the first one to explain regression to the mean. Regression to the mean is a concept that results will head towards the mean as the number of outcomes increases. This rule goes like trends of complex occurrences depend on different variables, where there is involvement of probability; average ones follow severe outcomes. Peter Bevelin explains with an example of John, who was not satisfied by the new employee's performance, and therefore he placed them in a program that would enhance their skills. They later increased their skills, and he concluded that the program increased made their skills better. Unfortunately, this is not necessarily the gospel truth. They might have improved their skills because of regression to the mean. Since the employees were rated as low performers, they would have increased their skills without the program, and it would have been due to many underlying reasons. Likewise, their poor skills would have been due to different reasons like fatigue, stress, or distractions. It could be that improvement is just a showcase of their true abilities.

We may have varied performance because of different reasons. Some extreme performance reduces the following period because the testing measurements are never exact. All measurements are part true and part error. If we make changes in our mode of performing things because of the recent unsuccessful events, we may increase our performance the next time despite our new mode of performance being equal or worse. It is the main reason why it is dangerous to use small samples to represent big data. It may also be the reason James March tells us that when we stay in our jobs for long, the less the difference between the record of performance and the actual performance. In regression to the mean, things keep changing in the short run. Its effects can be noticed in sports where we have unjustified speculations. Kahneman explains how a men's ski jump, a combination of two jumps, determines the final score. With his knowledge of the regression to the mean, he wondered why the sportsman from Norway became tense after his first great jump. It was because he was hoping to protect his position or doing worse. The other sportsman from Sweden had a bad jump at first, and he was relaxed because he had nothing to lose, and this motivates him to jump better. Kahneman states that the commentator also observed the regression mean and made a story to support it. Our situation above expounds on regression to the mean, which happens when there is a presence of luck like in our first example. Most of us attach our performance on lack, but in reality, the science involved is complex, and most of what we take as being in our control are random.

Relating the mean of regression to our situation above, a factor like wind can affect the performance of a jumper; if the wind is strong, it can make a good athlete perform poorly, and if the wind is favorable, a poor jumper may perform better. These effects wade, and the results regress to the normal conditions. Regression rule advises us to check on a person's track record when hiring rather than specific outcomes of a situation. In reality, if we have two people in the room who are 7 feet tall and the average height in the world is 5'6". This mean will reduce from 7 feet and get closer to the world mean of 5'6". In the mental model, regression to the mean mostly shows up in the world of sports, where we use a lot of statistics and numbers. In baseball, players can start the game batting at .500 and above, but as they continue to play more, their average decreases to .300. Regression to the mean also applies to gamble as well. A gambler will win a lot as he begins to play, but as he continues, he loses some winnings to the house. It is how casino houses set up their games. Let us look at the distribution curve below that points out how many times an experiment will produce a certain outcome. The highest part is the average, and you can notice how results group around it as they increase.

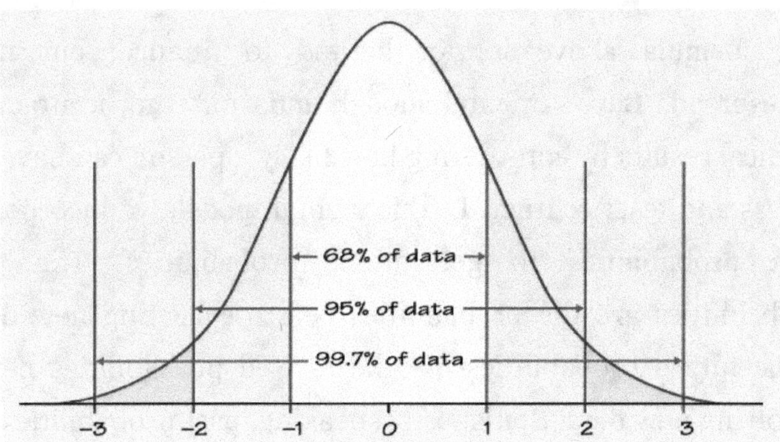

What Would Bayes Do (WWBD)?

Bayes' theorem determines conditional probability. It was named after a famous British mathematician Bayes Thomas.

The Formula For Bayes' Theorem Is

$$P(A|B) = \frac{P(A \cap B)}{P(B)} = \frac{P(A) \cdot P(B|A)}{P(B)}$$

where:

$P(A) =$ The probability of A occurring

$P(B) =$ The probability of B occurring

$P(A|B) =$ The probability of A given B

$P(B|A) =$ The probability of B given A

$P\left(A \cap B\right)) =$ The probability of both A and B occurring

The formula above is not limited to finance, but it is widespread. Baye's mental model finds out the accuracy of medical results by considering how likely a person can have the illness and test accuracy. In this mental model, we incorporate past probabilities to get future probabilities. The past probabilities are the probabilities before collecting new data, while future probabilities are the revised probabilities before involving new data. Statistically speaking, past probabilities are the probabilities of an outcome with the respect that outcome B has occurred. The formula can also be used to see how the probability of an outcome is affected by new information. For example, what is the probability of taking a King from a stack of cards? We have four kings in a 52 cards pack. Therefore the probability is 4/52, which is the same as 1/3 or 7.69%. Now, what would be the probability of getting a face card? The probability is 4/12 or 33.3% because we have 12 face cards in a pack of cards.

Let us look at an example of our model. We mentioned that our model follows conditional probability, which is the probability of an outcome on the condition that a second outcome occurred. We can ask ourselves what would be the probability of Amazon.com reduction in stock price. We can further ask ourselves what will be the probability of a reduction in Amazon's stock price with additional information that Dow Jones stock price reduced earlier. We can express this probability as P(AMZN) because the price has reduced ad P(DJIA) because the probability of Dow Jones and the price fell earlier. The conditional probability will be stated as Amazon stock price reduces because of the prior decrease in Dow Jones, which is equal to the probability that Amazon price falls and Dow Jones' falls because of the probability of a reduction in its index.

An example of deriving Bayes' mental model with an example

P(AMZN|DJIA) = P(AMZN and DJIA) / P(DJIA)

P(AMZN and DJIA) is the probability of *both* A and B occurring. This is also the same as the probability of A occurring multiplied by the probability that B occurs given that A occurrs, expressed as P(AMZN) x P(DJIA|AMZN). The fact that these two expressions are equal leads to Bayes' theorem, which is written as:

if, P(AMZN and DJIA) = P(AMZN) x P(DJIA|AMZN) = P(DJIA) x P(AMZN|DJIA)

then, P(AMZN|DJIA) = [P(AMZN) x P(DJIA|AMZN)] / P(DJIA).

In our formula above, P(AMZN) and P(DJIA) are Amazon's and Dow Jones' probabilities without a connection. This formula explains the connection of hypothesis before evidence as in Amazon's and the hypothesis after the evidence as in Dow Jones'. Let us find out more with a numerical example of the mental model.

Think of any drug test that has 95% accuracy. This means that this test shows 95% results on a person who is using it (true positive) and 95% on a person who is not using it (true negative). Now, our next assumption is that only 0.6% of the population uses the drug. If you were to choose an arbitrary positive test, we could use the following calculations to determine if the person is a drug user.

(0.95 x 0.006) / [(0.95 x 0.006) + ((1- 0.95) x (1 − 0.006))] = 0.0057 / (0.0057 + 0.0497) = 10.28%

Our model shows that even if you tested positive, a non-user is more likely to test positive that a user of the drug.

Do It like Darwin

Charles Darwin may have died in 1882, but his teachings can be used in today's' world. He wrote in not exact words that the species that survives is not the strongest nor the intelligent one, but the one responds to change most. Some people still argue that he did not write those words, but if you look at his works, you will conclude that they fit his thinking. He may have passed o before some titans in the business industry like Henry Ford or the Wright Brothers, but his work still applies in today's world. In 1986, Charlie Munger gave a short speech on what to avoid in life to be happy. He stated that Charles Darwin would be a middle scorer at Harvard that year, but we still recognize his works to date. Darwin's work violated all misery rules, and he always prioritized evidence to change the theory that he already had.

In contrast, today, people make early achievements and then go ahead to disconfirm information so that the results will be the same. Darwin's life is one that explains how a turtle can outrun a hare. E.O Wilson stated in his book that Darwin would have scored 130 in the IQ test. What lessons can we learn from Charles Darwin?

Extreme focus plus attentive energy

We can get our first idea from his autobiography, where he described some of his studies at Beagle. He states that the special studies were not as important as energetic industry habits and the concentration on his engagements. He pointed further that all he learned there were things he had seen and or about to see, and that habit continued for the next five years. He attributed his achievements to the training he acquired there. The habit of attending to the task in hand was also supported by Sherlock Holmes, Feynman, E.O. Wilson, and many others. Munger also commented that his success was due to the long attention span. According to Darwin, he had nothing relevant at hand. He had an extraordinary curiosity that made him search for data in the scientific field and by hand. From Darwin's study at Down House, he read a lot and made many notes. Over the years, he had a lot of interconnected facts. He searched for patterns and exceptions. He tested his theories on complicated organism groups such as orchids, primroses, and hominids. He thought broadly and took facts on many subjects, and at the same time, he thought carefully. Now, let us look at Munger's admiration for Darwin. He said that Darwin looked at exceptions to the last exceptions. He searched for the truth to avoid being wrong about reality. Darwin's study was not about the animal kingdom and plants. He went to the extent of studying his son, and from his notes, he wrote notes on the natural history of babies. He wondered if they start moving their muscles at the early stage of life. He also wondered if they wink and if you teach them at an early age if it was possible to avoid danger. As his child grew, he continued observing him and making notes. He wondered how his son realized that the reflection on the mirror was him. He wondered how he was able to differentiate that image in the mirror and the image of an actual person standing before him. All these were concluded on what he had seen and what he would likely see.

Become an expert

What can we learn from Darwin on becoming an expert? Darwin held Charles Lyell in high esteem. He described his mind as clear, sound judgment, cautious, and original because he made sure that he cleared all his doubts on geology and made him see things better than before. The second thing he admired in him is the warm sympathy he had on other scientists' work. When Darwin returned to England, he followed Lyell's example in Geology and collected all facts required in that subject. Darwin's study of geology gave him back up on conceptuality. Charles Darwin's work directed him to something new that species are of one family and evolve through variations and survive through natural selection. He explained that it was difficult for humans to come to that conclusion because we are slow in embracing change. Through the passages of Darwin, Munger prescribed the work required to hold a point of view. He stated that you must know the other side than the person holding it. When you do that, you harness your sight, unlike other people. We can conclude by saying that apart from good timing and good work, Darwin had a habit of completeness, accuracy, and diligence. He began with the correct ideas and focused on his reality. Finally, the best you can do is copy Darwin's mental habits, and they will serve you your whole life.

Think With System 2

So, what happens when I ask you what 1 + 1 is? Did you notice that you did not struggle, but the mind just gave you the answer? You did not even think about it. Let us see what will happen if I ask you what is 37 multiplied by 40? Not unless you are a genius, I am sure you need a calculator just like I do. In such a sum, you need to involve your reflective brain. Our reflexive brain is fast and concludes quickly while our reflective brain is slow and needs effort. Daniel Kahnemann names these two models as system one and system 2 for reflexive and reflective, respectively. Our system 1 operates with no effort, and it is quick. System 2 gives effort to the activities that require it and subjects it to concentration. These two do not exist in reality, but they are just models to help us understand our brain. These two systems are awake active every time you are awake; system 1 works automatically, while system 2 is in a comfortable and effortless mode. Our routine actions such as reading, talking are driven by system one, and system two only comes to play when you are encountered with something complex. This arrangement in our brain works well because system 1 does a good job, but on the downside, it is overconfident, and it sometimes does not delegate some decisions to system two, thereby creating errors. These errors are known as biases. Let us look at this diagram and read the words in them loudly.

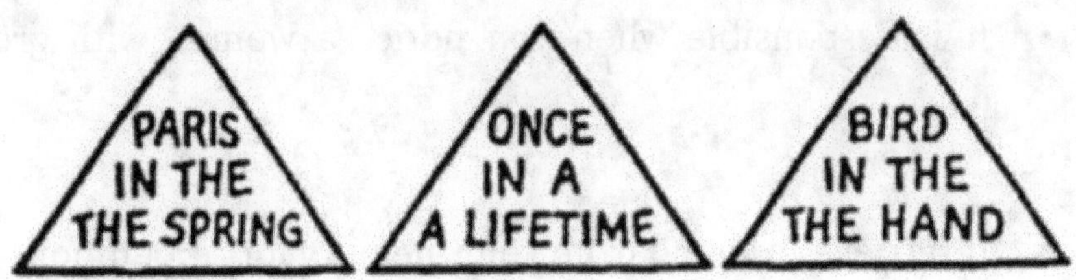

Did you notice any error? I know you didn't, but it is okay because not so many noticed it. In our first triangle, the word 'the' was written twice; in the second triangle, the word 'a' is repeated twice, and in the third triangle as well, the word 'the' is also repeated. What happened that made you not realize the mistake? Reading is automatic and does not require any effort. Remember, we mentioned that our system 1 is overconfident, and in a hurry to read the sentence, it overlooks small mistakes. If you pay attention, you will engage your system two, and you will perform better because your system two get disrupted if there is no attention.

System 2

System 2 is slow, infrequent, calculating, and effortless. What can it help you to do in life?

- It helps a person to stay ready before a sprint.

- It diverts your focus on the circus clowns.

- It makes you focus on the loud person at a party.

- It is responsible when you notice a woman with grey hair.

- It retrieves a sound from your memory for recognition.

- It helps you to maintain a faster pace than your normal rate.

- It concludes whether a behavior is appropriate or not in a social gathering.

- It is responsible for enabling you to count the letter 'a's' in a specific text.

- It is responsible for retrieving your number from your memory to give it to someone else.

- Do you know how difficult it is to park in a tight parking space? Well, system 2 helps you to do that.

- System 2 boosts of helping you to find out the price and quality ratio of two products.

- It helps you to solve complex calculations.

As we mentioned earlier, system two is the deliberate, rational, and analytical side of your brain. It is glued by the search of logic and more past information obtained through experiments and learning. System 2 processes data slowly and carefully by applying rules consciously, making the procedure to be demanding, but the outcome is better decisions. This system is usually engaged in case of uncertainties, complexities, or when you have ample thinking time, and the outcome has no margin for errors required. As slow and effortful as our system two is, it is not error-free. System two is not reliable when it is being used alone because it may slow down the process. This system relies on experience, which is not mean the outcome will be better performance. After all, experience devoid of feedback can breed faulty thinking.

Cognitive Reflection Test is designed to measure a person's ability to switch to system 2. Shane Frederick explains that in CRT, there are three easy items because they can be understood when explained, but to answer the tests, you need to come up with answers that come to mind at once. In this study, he explains that as we proceed to answer questions from the third one, we reduce the use of our intuition. It is also biased because it states that male participants performed better. Judges in the US have used CRT. They are said to use intuition to get clues that lead them to a decision that they later change to logic. This study showed that only two out of three judges gave thought through answers to the three questions. This confirmed that the remaining judges relied on system 1 to make decisions. These decisions are not a general conclusion on how judges make their judgments in court, but it is important to make the judges aware of their thinking and regulate it, especially system two, that can expose their biases.

Chapter 3: Eye-Opening Problem-Solving

It is a common phenomenon of human beings trying to solve the daily problems solely with their minds. However, the solutions to the problems that present to an individual's life often have a deep root as the solution. The most advised method to go about life problems is finding a breakthrough in thoughts and patterns of living. It is a difficult task for these factors of change to come about by looking at them as a short-term form of approach.

Successful people have the tendency of reweaving the problems they encounter with a view of a long term perspective. The befit of this kind of metal setting is it makes it easy to arrive at solutions. These solutions often have the potential of making an individual be happy in his or her life. A good depiction is a person who is looking to find a job with his or her aim to improve his or her happiness. However, there is a certain reason that could be detrimental to an individual if he or she uses it as the reason to find a job. The reason is pursuing a job to fulfill what is socially right and not what his or her interests are.

The other depiction would be that of a parent who is aiming to settle his or her daughter. The major aim of this act is to make his or her girl settle. However, there are cases where it is a disaster for a girl who needs independence. The reason is the act has the potential of causing her more problems when she is married. This makes her parents find themselves in a situation that is helpless than where they were before. These two depictions prove the element that the solutions to a problem are supposed to be able to increase and individual happiness. The solution is also supposed to go a notch higher to improving an individual's soul empowerment and ascension to a level that is peaceful for his or her existence.

There is a certain analogy that is used to describe the process of solving problems using the third eye. The analogy is using objectiveness like God to solve his or her problems. One is supposed to be able to open his or her third eye because it creates a good connection to other realms of solving problems. It might sound overwhelming, but the two physical eyes are only tasked with the role of seeing the physicality of the world. The third eye is tasked with the role of seeing the information that is non-physical. This includes different interpretations of life happenings. One can describe the third eye-opening as the center of intuition. Opening this eye requires several things, such as:

Peer Review Your Perspectives

The normal life of a human being has nothing that is right or wrong with regard to rare circumstances put aside. Right and wrong tend to be relative terms with regards to the side an individual wants to go. The common school of thought is that success is doing what one loves until the end of life. These are major destinations an individual has to reach. However, there is an element that several people tend to miss it. The element is that the two terms of right and wrong are what is used to approach the journey for an individual to be successful.

One is discouraged from thinking the two words are the destination for the journey of being successful. A person is termed successful in the event that he or she is walking a journey that he or she is always learning and growing from it. Successful people do what they love in the event that they see every moment that presents itself to them as an opportunity. There are billions of human beings that are in existence currently. This makes the view of the opportunity to be different among them. Therefore, it is important for an individual to be able to find his form of opportunity.

The millennial we are currently living is filled with peers who are frustrated nearly every day. The cause of frustration is the thought of everything seeming to look like being permanent. You are not supposed to wine about the cubicle kind of job you have and having the end thought of sticking there. This is detrimental because it diminishes your desire to be successful. It is very important for any person who is seeking to be successful in being able to realize that there are lessons in the journey of life. It is also important to embrace these lessons. Embracing mistakes makes a person be able to reach the absolute state of being successful. The sense behind it is that a person will be growing effortlessly to becoming a better version of himself or herself.

There is a major reason why several people tend to suffer when it comes to a review of thoughts. It is because of the accountability factor that is involved in them. Accountability involves an individual looking at the reflection of his or her thoughts. The process is important because it has the potential of shifting blames on different problems of life to ownership. You are supposed to be able to see opportunities from the trouble that life presents and an individual from this process. It is a theory that can be used across all the angles of life from social, academic to work-life of an individual.

You are supposed to able to have a leaser focus on the lessons from a life event. This brings the school of thought that an individual is not supposed to think about the problem. Try not to blame people around you as the cause of the problems that you experience in your daily life. Every situation that life has the potential of fixing an individual has the potential of being a turnaround. These lessons are often found everywhere, and it is a person's task to be able to spot them. They have the potential of making an individual grow. When it becomes a difficult task to find the lessons in this technique, an individual can be able to ask those who are around him or her by asking them questions about what he or she can improve in his or her life. The major aim is always to be able to change your perspective.

Find Your Own Flaws

There are certain forms of thinking that fill the normal world of an individual. You are subjected to think of having a successful business or a generally successful life. There are other factors that dominate the fantasy world of an individual. These other factors are winning the lottery every day, having a good form of hair, and a fantastic tummy that is flat.

However, there is an imperfect world that you are supposed to be able to deal with as an individual. The fact that we face every day is that we are only good at certain things. There are other things that you make them passable and some things that are downright lousy despite being important. It can be very difficult to handle the factual truth that you can be able to handle everything perfectly. Or on other terms, it is impossible to be a perfect human. The common thought is that of a person who is the head of an organization. This person is prone to having the thought of he or she is the only person who can make an organization to be achieving its goals and targets optimally. This thought is fallacious if you are such kind of person because no one is perfect, neither is any human being.

It is important for you to find your flaws because no one is perfect. The process of being successful goes a notch higher to turning them into forms of strengths. There are several steps you can follow for you to be able to be successful in turning these weaknesses into several forms of strength.

1. Recognition of the Weaknesses

It is a difficult task of turning weaknesses into strength in the event that you deny them. Therefore, the first task is accepting that you have flaws and finding a way of spotting them. There are several ways to spot these forms of weaknesses, and the most common one is taking a personality test. It is a complicated and tricky process when it comes to navigating through it. It is one of the most validated methods across the globe. The process has the tendency to test and group human beings into five popular personalities. The process is focused on five key areas of your personality. They referred to personality areas such as neuroticism, agreeableness, extroversion, consciousness, and openness.

2. Get Guidance

It is important always to have a constant thought that not every person can be trusted. Opening up about your weakness is a delicate issue, and you are required to have a person you have a close relationship with. The person who you are to open up about these issues has to be bright and intelligent. This will give you a better insight into how to deal with this kind of problem. Such people can act as mentors since they give you guidance to achieve your goals in life, which are a measure of success. These people can be friends, family members, or colleagues you interact with at a personal level.

3. Being Prepared

There are moments where you can be able to fight weakness you possess in an easy way. The efficient and easy method entails getting excellent forms of preparation. A good depiction would be that of a person who has a problem of getting lost moments he or she travels by himself or herself. Such a person can overcome the weakness of forgetting direction by making sure he or she has a map any moment he or she is traveling. This entails the usage of paper maps or GPS applications on either his or her car, tablet, or phone. The same case can be used by you when you are at work or at school. This entails looking for more information about the situation you are about to handle or the person who will be involved in it.

4. Hire the Skills You Lack

Successful is known for acknowledging that they are no perfect at everything they do. This makes them have a low likely hood of handling things that they do not know. Therefore, the rich are known for going the extra mile of hiring people to fulfill the tasks that they are not good at executing them. The process is advantageous because despite compensating a person's weakness, it provides him with new ideas that he or she can use to better him or herself. You are supposed to be able to delegate several tasks of your life to other people around you. The tasks would be done efficiently in the event that an individual goes a notch higher to empowering those people who are around him or her to be able to perform these tasks with ease.

5. Getting Just Good Enough

At this point, you are able to realize that you are not good at all the tasks you perform. However, there are other tasks that can be learned on a daily basis. They can be incorporated with the tasks you already know. The next step would be you going a notch high to make sure that you better yourself in both the new skills. And the other quality attributes that you use to possess. The process of getting to be good enough will help you get through certain problems in life that seem to be very difficult. Take an example of an entrepreneur using general knowledge of entrepreneurship principles to get through situations where technology has failed, such as market analysis. The process is advantageous because it makes a person be able to have a smart approach in everything he or she does in his or her life.

6. Looking for a Way to Serve Other People With the Same Problem

There is a common statement that has an ideology of invention being born from aggravation. This means that for you to be able to gain certain skills in your life, you need calamities to strike first. It is a hidden form of converting weaknesses into strength. Taking a look at the rich people who have several forms, innovations will make you have an intriguing discovery. The interesting discovery would be that these people made their fortune from the aim of helping society. This is irrespective of service or product that they introduced in the market. Having a keen look at your weaknesses can serve as an opportunity since it has the potential of leading you to a successful venture.

Separate Correlation From Causation

Causation and correlation can seem to look like two similar terms with a blurry line. However, recognizing the difference between the two can be very important for you. This is because it will help you to break down your efforts on factors in life that have low value. The process is important because nearly the whole world is focused on concentrating on factors that have a high value. It can take any shape such as skills, product, and service or a personality trait.

The truth is that that correlation and causation have the probability of being in existence at the same time. However, from the above information, causation does not mean correlation. It is important for a person to know the difference between the two terms. Causation can be described as the resulting action from action has been done. For example, action A leading to action B. On the other hand, correlation can be described as the resulting relationship between two actions. A depiction would be the relationship of action A to B. These actions or events are not subjected to be the cause of the other when finding their correlation.

There is a certain reason that explains why human beings have a hard task of differentiating the two aspects of thinking. The major reason is that the human mind is fixed to finding several patterns in life, even in the event that they do not exist. You are prone to fabricating certain patterns in the event that two variables appear to have a close association. The close association formed by the mind makes these life happenings to seem like they are dependent on each other. It is the reason why humans are prone and quick to implying the cause and effect relationship. This is in the event that there is a dependent resulting in an independent event on the other hand.

 This act has a detrimental effect on individual success. The major reason is that it can lead you to a path of erroneous conclusion when you are executing tasks such as factor analysis. Correlation is a statistic tool when it comes to factor analysis. The technique is tasked with the role of depicting the level of relatedness between two variables. It is normal to find that two variables do not have a similar cause or effect; this is despite the variables having a close relationship.

It brings to limelight another description that can be used to refer to causation. The description is causation is the connection that exists between the effect and cause of certain actions. There are several depictions that can be used to illustrate this phenomenon. They include a person claiming that the process of him or her walking through the door was the reason he or she broke his or her nose. The other probable cause would be he or she was texting or using his or her phone while walking. Therefore, in this context, texting and the event of the nose breaking would be the reason why the person broke her or his nose.

There are other phenomena that happen each and every day that you can be able to relate. Take the example of looking at the cause of accidents. Performing a factor analysis requires you to have several considerations. They might include red cars, higher speed limits, inclement weather, and young drivers. You can be subjected by the mind to thinks that red cars have the tendency of causing accidents, which is not the case. Taking a look at young drivers sparks the use of statistics that claim young drivers have the potential of causing accidents. However, this is not the direct link of all the road carnages that are experienced. The two factors prove it hard to categorize them as causation or correlation.

You can take a deep look at the weather and try to classify it as either causation or correlation. Rain can have the potential of making a young driver cause an accident because of poor visibility. However, it is not the direct cause of all the accidents that are experienced. Rain can make roads to be slippery and give a driver a difficult task to break, but it is not the force behind making two vehicles to collide. Taking a look at high speed has the potential of making a person cause an accident, and it is risky. However, the issue for the accident happening would be malfunctioning of the breaks that are a direct lead to accidents.

The process of understanding causation and correlation is a mastered art by successful people. It is a beneficial way of looking at daily life problems that present an individual. The advantage is it helps a person to avoid making incorrect assumptions based on the data one has. You can be able to influence people around you, including yourself, by looking through the critical lenses provided by this analysis. It can be a difficult task of you looking at several life happenings solely at the correlating factors. It becomes very difficult to find several solutions to certain problems. Therefore, achieving success in your life requires you to use data as the determining factor of the cause so as to focus on the highest impact success can bring.

Storytelling in Reverse

The other common way that is used to refer to this act is a backward form of planning. There are moments that your boss can call or message you that he or she wants to talk to you on the following day in the morning. The reason might be about the great idea you pitched to him or her during the day in a meeting. The probable phenomenon is that your brain will reach a point where it will be firing several forms of cylinders. The reason behind this is that a person will be looking to seek a new plan of how to formulate the idea. It entails searching for several materials or facts that are supportive of the idea. It goes a notch higher to you being able to look for the best way you can be presentable in a more professional way.

The most probable question that will cross your mind would be how to formulate this plan. It can be confusing when you seek to find the best place to start your idea. It would be starting from where the meeting ended or thinking from the results to where the future and the present converge. The situation might sound to be triggering arbitrary questions. However, there is research that was conducted on the issue by the School of Business at Korea University. The findings of the research said that the path an individual chooses for his or her success has a major influence on the desired outcome.

Several successful people use backward form planning. The major reason is to be able to achieve optimum results on their objectives. Backward planning has several prove that it has been used to prove that it has a high potential of leading to high levels of success. The researchers who were investigating this issue used several series of studies. The process involved asking several participants to plan for a special meeting or event. These events were things, such as launching a product or meeting with the boss.

The other study being carried entailed tasking students with a specific role. The task was about planning for their exams in two optional ways, which were either in reverse or chronological order. Results for these participants who were students were compared. They were merited against their methods of planning. The findings of this research were intriguing since those who planed backward had a better performance, unlike the student who had a forward plan.

The best thing about planning backward is it keeps the goal to be at sight. It is despite the time frame that is allocated for the achievement of the goals set. The reason why the other set of students were able to achieve their goals and overcome the huddle of the exam was that they were able to realize what their goal was. The act makes it easy for an individual to be able to attain his or her goal with ease because it is considered close and attainable.

There was also another finding that was established, which was brought as a result of being able to plan backward. The findings were this form of doing or solving life events makes it clear to have functional steps. They claimed that the process made them feel more confident about the types of choices they had set to be able to achieve their form of success.

The process of planning backward can be very advantageous in your life. It might sound overwhelming on which kind of life situation it can be perfectly be applied. This entails gathering the right documents for the right research and talking with a close friend before making a pitch of your idea to people who are in the board room. This does not stop at the workplace since there are certain ideas that are supposed to be planed earlier when it comes to educational and family issues.

There are several problems that you can face in your day to day life. These problems are well-sorted is you are in a position of finding solutions first. It makes it easy for you to solve the problem since you will be tasked with finding possible ways to find the probability that is the solution. An example would be in the event you did not have a good performance on the examination results. You are supposed to set a target for your next score then looking for solutions such as changing the time table or ways of studying. This is a simple way of solving a problem by looking first at the solution and then solving the problem. It is has been used by various successful people across the globe.

SCA

This model of identification and solving a problem is commonly used in successful organizations. The method is described as the use of symptom cause and action. This is the reason for the term SCA, referring to the Symptom Cause Action model. There are certain problems you have heard an individual being told that the problem will have a solution in the event; there is a reversal of a process. These comments are common when the problem is related to a high focus on the strategic facilitator. This system used for solving problems was developed by the Process Iceberg Organization. It is a good form of identification of certain life problems since you are able to facilitate the emotional side. It entails the identification of negative emotions and working the way up to find solutions from them.

Get Back to First Principles

Several successful people from the old and the current ages have been able to achieve their forms of success by investing a lot of time in their work. The character of putting more working hours on a worthy cause has the potential of making problems that would likely present themselves, have an easy way of being dealt with. This is the major reason why you can have the potential of questioning how successful people have the potential of achieving so much within a short life span. The questions are prone to piling up to a level of asking oneself how these people manage all their activities and the secret behind their success.

A good depiction in the current world would be that of Mr. Ellon Musk. He is a tech guru who was able to spot several problems and created a financial service known as PayPal, an automotive and Transportation Company. The answer behind these massive forms of success is simple. You are supposed to be able to read. Reading plays a very important role in an individual's life. You are able to improve your inner creativity by reading extensively. This comes in handy when you are executing several activities since it opens up your genius mind.

Researching more about a problem has an effect on changing an individual's perspective on the issue. The common term that is used to describe this phenomenon is the power of compounding. Having adequate knowledge of a life problem has the potential of paying certain forms of interest. Having a thinking mind that is anchored on the first principle has the potential of giving you solutions that are innovative on problems that are hard.

The brain is fixed to thinking that the use of analogies is the best way to view the happenings of life. The wiring of the brain portrays this thinking as a safe way of thinking. It is not a difficult task when it comes to breaking this pattern of thinking. It requires you to be able to take several steps back and begin to think about the basic principles.

This entails the usage of the first principle to be able to build on the blocks of true knowledge. This principle is important because it is the best way that an individual can be able to reverse life problems that are complicated. The process requires you to be able to break down to basic elements that reassemble with each other from the root. The technique is beneficial to you because you will be able to think on your own. The advantage goes to a higher level of making an individual be able to unchain the artistic potential you possess. This is very important when you are aiming to move to a direction that is aligned with the objectives you have set.

The process of using the first principle is easy as it is simply finding fundamental parts of a problem. You are supposed to go on a different level; this entails being able to find the problem so as to see the issue on bare-bones as it is. You are warned from confusing axioms and analogy during this process. It forms a goes base of reasoning when you have the constituent parts of the problem. The process is effective when you are able to set changes and improvements that are recognizable.

Chapter 4: Anti-Mental Models: How Avoidance Breeds Success

Avoid Direct Goals

There are no right ways of setting goals. In other words, there are no formulas that are set to guide in the art of setting goals. However, depending on the value as well as the issue at hand, goal setting becomes vital. However, there are various aspects that one ought to consider before setting goals. For example, one ought to avoid the art of setting goals that are direct. In most cases, direct goals are lagging and tend to be delaying. Such goals may cause one to lose focus and start concentrating on other things. In other words, if you set goals that are lagging, there are chances that you will overstay before the realization of the goals. It is worth noting that a direct goal means that no one else has the power of changing your action or rather the choice you have made. In other words, whatever you do has immediate actions and measurable impact on a person's life. The art of setting direct goals is critical. However, it is wise to consider the effects that they might have on the future. The art is linked to the fact that any action that you take has a great impact on the result of the goal. In most cases, if you fail to realize the dream well, there are chances that it might collapse. In other words, in case you make a mistake as you explore your own goals, there are chances that you may fail in the long –run. The art is linked to the fact that your actions have a direct impact on the realization of the goal.

For you to be successful and achieve greatness, you need to have laid out goals. There is no great as well as a successful person who make history without having set goals in their life. When you lay out the goals, you will have a vision that you will work hard to achieve. You will push yourself to make sure that you will get the best out of what you have set. When you have a goal, you will never wait and look for things to happen. When you have something to measure what you do against, you will try to improve so that there will be positive results. Setting goals will help you work hard to make sure that your work will translate to something tangible. Don't just work hard because you have to, and there is nothing you are aiming to achieve. Setting goals makes you strive for higher. Even if you miss your target, you will have done something constructive and worth it. Goals will force you to be more active than you should have been if you had not set any. Know what you need to have in a specific period so that you can have something to stand with. You will think ahead of everything, and that will help you to create an action plan. When things don't go per your project, you will be in a position to review as well as adjust the arrangements to have a better chance to implement it to the best. Head in a direction that will work for the vision that you have. Goals are created in two ways: in mind, and then that will translate to the physical world. The mental part of it will happen when you set clear goals. The material will come to being when you work towards making the goals a reality. Without the mental part of it, there will be the physical manifestation of the goals. The first step you need to take is setting clear goals, and you will see that your dreams will come true. That is the moment that things will start falling in place.

For instance, assuming your direct goal is a bull's eye. In case you throw a dart and fail to focus on the bull's eye, there are chances that you will miss. Whether the arrow hits the board or not, the fact remains that your actions are against your goal hence a fail. In most cases, one is forced to take a different dimension or rather a trial. There are cases where even after trying, the results are the same, and failure is noted. In such cases, one requires a complete resetting of goals. In most case, the re-adjustment tend to be costly as it is not a guarantee that one will hit the target. In other words, even after the second trial, one may fail and miss the target as well.

The other demerit of setting direct goals is that a lot of human effort is required for one to excel. In other words, the building of direct goals requires the individual bearing the dream to actively participate in the action of building it. The aspect is linked to the fact that he or she is the vision bearer and knows what is needed. In most cases, when they fail to be present in the process of building the goal, the chances are that all that they had built collapses at once. In most cases, they are the prime decision-makers. In other words, they are the sole-trader and make decisions without consulting others. It is worth noting that even if they may require support from others, they remain to be the monopolies of their goal such that anything that has to be done is dependent on their directions. In that, they offer clear guidelines over what needs to be done. Thus, it is wise to consider other goals rather than direct goals. The aspect is linked to the fact that if the directives offered fails to work, there are chances that the individual will have no one to question. In other words, the losses that are incurred are beard by a similar person. However, in cases of profits or rather gains, the amusement remains with the goal setter.

The art of sharing ideas is important. In other words, if you are setting goals, it is wise to set goals that are relevant. In most cases, the art of consulting is never bad. In other words, you may require a helping hand in terms of what you think. In other words, as you excel, you may require an individual who will help you rise and guide you over the realization of your goals. The aspect is linked to the fact that there are people who might have excels in the field you are exploring, and you may need their advice. However, the art of avoiding their advice may cost you in the long run. In other words, you may fall in a ditch that may cost all your dreams as well as investments. For instance, if you are dreaming of winning a larger business mall in the city, you may require to hear some pieces of advice from those who have been working in the city so as you may capture the attention of a good number of people in the center. In other words, there is no way you can learn about the marketing of a place without necessarily seeking information from those who had excelled long before you had the idea. In most cases, they offer the best forms of ideas that may save a person`s mind. However, the art of setting direct goals prevents any intervention. In other words, direct goals encourage the art of avoiding other people's minds to avoid confusion. It is worth noting that the art of setting goals is important. However, seeking advice or including other people`s efforts is vital. It increases the manner in which the goal is achieved. There are chances that after the art of setting goals, you may require an individual who has similar aims or rather dreams to actualize your vision. In other words, there are people who are good at laying down strategies that are aimed at achieving goals. Such people are required for the actualization of such dreams. However, the art of setting direct goals may hinder their art of excelling. The art is linked to the fact that direct goals are more into individual ambitions.

Avoid Thinking Like an Expert

The art of thinking is essential in any form of success. Thinking opens an individual's mind and helps in deliberating over specific issues. It is worth noting that life can be challenging and at times, draining. However, there is a dire need to deliberate on matters with care.

In most cases, the carelessness that is common among individuals is brought about by the lack of putting some sense of thinking about the future or rather aspects that ought to be done to avoid complications. In the world, different disciplines are explored in life. Since people are different, they tend to explore the subjects that favors them in life. In other words, the art of specialization allows people to follow their dreams to be experts. Most of these experts are "know it all individuals." They tend to specialize and explore their field of interest to the latter. Most of them have vast experiences over some regions of life hence the art of being called experts. Most of them are the teachers or rather the guides who offer guidelines to individuals. The aspect is critical in the sense that it allows people to seek information from them and get assistance. There are cases where these experts get proud of their achievements, and they tend to disregard others. Also, there are cases where their level of expertise becomes so high that they don't see the need to seek more information. The attitude turns against them, and especially they lack the necessary support that is required. Thus, the minds of an expert are always full, and they, at times, develop some detrimental characters. In other words, they tend to disregard others and fail to see the need to seek more information.

If you want to excel, you need to stop thinking like an expert. In other words, there is no need to assume you know everything, yet you don't own the earth. It is worth noting that life is a journey full of challenges, and there is no way you can fully meet all your needs. Even in the world of business, some people have excelled in the industry and have succeeded. However, before they realize, they had to pass via many aspects of life that shape them.

In most cases, if they had refused to learn and grasp ideas from those who were ahead of them, there are chances that they would have failed. In the same way, if you want to succeed in life, ensure that you avoid thinking like an expert. The art is linked to the fact that you may assume some of the information or slight advice that might take you to greater heights. In other words, people who don't think like experts are always consulting. Before making any decision, it is good to be wise and consider what other people know. The aspect is linked to the fact they might be having ideas well as strategies that might help you improve. However, experts think that they are the best and fail to include views of people who might be helpful.

Take a look at some of the behaviors that prevent experts from succeeding

Pride

There is a particular adage that claims that feelings of pride come before a fall. In other words, people who are pride tend to fail in the long-run. The aspect is linked to the fact that these people avoid situations where they will be confronted and distracted. In other words, their decisions are final, and they don't like listening to what other people claim or think. Some experts are very proud of themselves to the point of distracting others.

In most cases, they only desire to be recognized and be given the uttermost recognition. In other words, most of them are a narcissist. They are the kind of people who manipulate others because of the things they have. They might be knowing certain aspects of life. The element causes them to be manipulative as they seek more attention. Since most of these people are influential, failure to submit to their orders may cost you the job or rather your reputations. Thus, you need to be careful when dealing with them. Therefore, if you want to be successful in life, you don't have to behave or think as experts do. The aspect is linked to the fact that you will be proud and, in the long run, fail to seek information even from your seniors. You might have issues when dealing with your juniors as they may fail to offer their efforts in helping you due to your pride. There are cases where they may even allow you to fall into a ditch as hey watch. However, if you are humble, the chances are that all categories of people will have time to speak to you. Through their efforts, you will have time to comprehend about other issues that are important in life. In other words, you will be able to grasp some information that is vital in life. The aspect is linked to the fact that knowledge is power, and this power lies within the confines of individuals. Thus, if you want to excel in anything, you need to style up and talk to people. They might be having some of the details you need to excel. However, if you adopt the minds of an expert, you will assume you and later realize that you comprehended nothing. For instance, if you were venturing into a new business, you need to seek information from people who have explored such business or people who have been in the market for long. Such people add value to someone in the long run. There are times where experts think that they know everything. What happens is that they assume that their decision is final — such mindsets block other individuals from reaching them out.

In most cases, underestimate the ideas from others and end up failing. Thus, as you start your journey to success, don't ignore the input that other people might have. You need to be vigilant and open-minded such that you can allow other people to seek you and share out their ideas in your life.

Limited Flexibility

In life, many issues happen. There are different challenges that people face every day. In most cases, the way people strike some of these challenges determines their level of success. Expert, in most cases, is very rigid when it comes to the art of changing ideas. In other words, they are not flexible, especially when it comes to change. They are the kind of people who will remain with their opinion whether it is working out or not. They might die with the mind that their purpose is the best and will work out in the best way possible.

In most cases, the sensation causes them to fail, yet they could have agreed to buy ideas from other people and succeed. For instance, if they decide on selling a certain kind of product, they may be so conservative and fail to change their ideas even if they are making a loss. In other words, they fear or hatred being corrected. However, you don't have to adopt such a mindset. The aspect is linked to the fact that there are times when your ideas fail, and you might be forced to change. You don't have to be rigid and fail in the long run. Live with an open mind and accept to hear what other people say. You might be having information about something. However, that should not deter you from seeking more information that seems relevant.

In most cases, there are no aspects that are complex to everyone. In other words, there is a situation that might prove difficult for you. In most cases, such conditions might appear simpler to other people. Thus, you need to speak out your mind and deliberately seek information from others. You don't have to behave as if you know every aspect of life.

Adoption of Patterns

Most experts have acquired specific patterns that work in their life. In other words, experience has taught them some aspects that are critical in life at large. Most of them have great ideas on how to solve specific issues of life. The element is crucial in the sense that it allows them to stick to their mindo-set no matter the change s they have. The aspect is linked to the fact that they have worked in some of these areas, and they have complete knowledge of what needs to be done for one to excel. However, there are times where such ideas fail. There are cases where their competitions or rather challengers adapt to the pattern they have. In such situations, all the efforts of the experts fail to succeed. However, most of them tend to avoid adopting other means, thinking that their methods will work out for them. The rigidness may, at times, cost them dearly, especially if their plans fail to work out. Thus, as you plan or instead start your success journey, it is good to consider several aspects. You don't have to identify patterns and stick to them to the latter, especially if they don't work. In other words, if the plans or the strategies laid fail to work, you don't have to kill yourself. You can come up with new strategies that will help you solve the issue in other ways. In other words, different means can be used to succeed in life. Even after failing, life has to continue. Thus, you don't have to be a fool who does a similar thing expecting different results.

Complexity

In life, one ought to be simple. There is no need for being involved in terms of thinking as well as the verge of doing things. In other words, it is, at times, suitable to utilize the simple things that are vital in life. The aspect means that, for you to succeed, it is not a must you be complex. However, you can strategize on ensuring that all things are working despite the art of using simple tactics. Experts, at times, believe in complexity. In other words, they think that for them to succeed, there is a dire need to be complicated and avoid direct means of achieving things. They prefer using complicated formulas to solve problems. However, the aspect might be detrimental if the plan fails to work out. In other words, there are cases where experts use complicated means to achieve things and end up failing. Most of them are determined to keep using the method to maintain their level of expertise. However, you don't have to use similar strategies to excel. In other words, if there are means that are relevant and available, you don't have to tire your minds thinking like an expert that it will work out. You need to be vigilant and avoid the art of being rigid. The aspect is detrimental as it prevents one from utilizing other people`s ideas that may work-out for them.

Avoid Your Non-Genius Zones Avoid To-Do Lists

Your zone of genius is your unique power. In other words, it is a kind of quality that brings your life into work and allows different aspects of life to be better than others. It relates to self-limiting beliefs that keep us from pursuing careers as well as the things we are meant for. Such jobs are critical in the sense that they allow us to be joyful and more enthusiastic about what we do. In other words, if you can do or a career of your choice, chances are that you will lead a life full of joy and fulfillment. When you lay out a plan, you are in short connecting with your innermost desires. When that happens, you will feel motivated and having something you are working to achieve. That will help you if you are in a position that is easy to compromise.

In most cases, careers tend to utilize our gifts rather than the efforts that one may put. The Non-Genius Zones are the areas where your efforts are required for certain things to be accomplished. In most cases, there is a more significant leap when the zone of genius is utilized to deliberate on issues. The aspect is linked to the fact that less energy and will power is required. In other words, the deliberation is more natural hence the minimal utilization of energy and will power. However, it is worth noting that success isn't achieved overnight. One requires to work deliberately will all zones to be successful.

In life, various aspects require our human effort. For instance, if you have a dream of becoming a doctor, you need to be passionate. In other words, the doctor aspect ought to lie within you. The element allows one to be successful and feel fulfilled in life. The art is linked to fewer efforts, or preferably energy is used. However, there are situations where we find ourselves in the non-genius zones. In such a time, there are a lot of things that one outline that ought to be done for one to be successful. In other words, there is a list of things that one outlines to fit in the zone. For instance, there is a desire to work hard as well as thinking positively, that allows individuals to keep working. However, it is good to avoid such a list and deliberate on seeking an opportunity that is aimed at exploring and locating success.

Take a look at the reasons as to why you need to avoid such a list.

Limiting your Efforts

In every situation, some aspects require self –deliberation or instead of being worked upon for the result to be great. However, it is worth noting that when one is in a non-genius zone, there are things that ought to be done. For instance, one may be forced to thinking positively or rather work extra harder. There are people who, at a time, seek formulas that help them excel. The to-do list offers a temporary solution that provides success. However, it is self-limiting. The aspect is linked to the fact that after working on specific issues, there are chances that one may find themselves in the same situation.

In most cases, one may be forced to use the same formulas rather than thinking of other possibilities. The reason behind all these actions is that one is operating in non-genius zones. In other words, the individual is working in a field that is different from what he or she is meant for. In other words, if one is intended to be a teacher, and by default, they end up being doctors, there are chances they will be forced to work extra harder for them to achieve success. In such situations that they will be forced to make a list aimed at helping them achieve success. However, there are times where such plans fail to work; in such a situation, the perceived aspects fail to work. Thus, you need to be deliberate and avoid limiting yourself.

Creates a Comfort Zone

The art of creating a list that ought to be followed tend to offer a comfort zone in life. The aspect prevents one from being creative. In most creativity attracts failure in life. The element is linked to the fact that from time to time, issues get to arise. There are at times where such problems tend to emerge, and the formulas or strategies tend to fail. In such situations, loses are incurred as in the comfort zone; things tend to be different. In other words, people rarely think when they are in a comfort zone.

Avoid the Path of Least Resistance

In life, there are various challenges. Life can be challenging at times, and one ought to make tough decisions. The aspect means that there are different paths that one can take. In other words, in life, there is a smooth as well as a resistance path. Most people who like living in comfort zones prefer taking routes that are less resistance. The other aspect is linked to the fact that such a way allows people to be content. However, people who avoid such roads tend to set goals that are alarming. In other words, the goals tend to be challenging and keep the theme at toes. It is worth noting that when you set goals, it will make you be an accountable person. You will not talk, but you will have an obligation to act and work towards achieving the set goals. You will not be responsible to anyone, but to yourself, since you are the one who has set the goals and you need to see the results. That will be so because no one is aware that you have some set goals. You need to know that no one will have again when you achieve what you have set. You are the one who will be on the safe side when you do everything according to what you have laid out. When you have something that you are looking forward to achieving, you will establish whether you are on the right track. If you notice that you are not heading in the right direction, you will adjust and know what to do so that you can have an achievement in a given time. You will feel obliged to achieve what you have to so that you will not fail yourself. You will be in a position to monitor your performance while you are working intending to get to your target. If you fall short, you will know the action plan to take so that you will address the whole issue to get the results you aim for. You will do away with all the activities that waste your time and work on the goals as an accountable person.

Thus, if you want to excel in life, set goals that are challenging in life. The aspects allow one to work hard and avoid the art of being content — the aspect call for one to deliberate on different issues aimed at excelling. The art of preventing the less resistance path allows one to eliminate the things that are not important and what that does not help in achieving your goals. Prioritize as well as identifying what you need to take so that you can make your goals. When you do that, you will get the maximum results. For you to be successful and achieve greatness, you need to have laid out goals. There is no great as well as a successful person who make history without having set goals in their life. When you lay out the goals, you will have a vision that you will work hard to achieve. You will push yourself to make sure that you will get the best out of what you have set. Most of these people move out of their comfort zones hence the art of succeeding.

Chapter 5: Oldies But Goldie's: They Are Still Around for a Reason

Murphy's Law

We will first begin our discussion with a recap of the origin of Murphy's Law. Murphy's Law draws its origin or is stated that it originated from a north base air force base back in 1949. History has it that it was given its name after the famous Edward. A Murphy. This was an engineer who was at the time working on a project. This project was purposed to bring out the feedback of the amount of pressure that an individual can put up with say an aircraft decides to crash. In his venture, he once encountered a piece of machinery known as a transducer, which was had been fixed in a defective manner. After quite an observation, he decided to swear that if there was a way in which it could be done in a wrong manner, he would unearth it. This was the main reason why the contractor kept a list of laws, and in it, he decided to encompass this particular phrase known as Murphy's Law. The implication of this particular law was an effect of an ancient law that has now been given form and meaning. In the next few years, Murphy's Law gained fame and was quoted by various individuals, not only but to mention Dr. John Paul Stapp. This was the onset of aerospace manufacturers picking it up and commencing to utilize it.

Murphy's Law draws its basis from a particular set of laws known as sod laws. Murphy who was an individual, was drawing sense to what the sods had already talked about. Murphy's Law draws its basis from Sod's law, and in this sense, it tends to send it its regards because this would be unfair to any sod. The law of the Sods is one that has stood the taste of the time in that its existence surpasses that of a man. Therefore talking about Murphy's Law and failing to mention Sod's law is almost as catastrophic. Sod's laws have been given relevance b the Yorkshire families, and thus it keeps being passed through most English jurisdictions. The original name of sod's law keeps on diminishing because the name is no longer recognized, and what people draw relevance to is cursory. Murphy's Law encompasses nothing that is insulting or has nothing which diminishes the law of the Sods. The idea is that this type of logic would not have been unearthed late in this century.

The most distinguishing factor about Murphy's Law is that it was formulated by another individual who is not murphy. This individual is known as Michael. This is another perception that has also been adopted aborted the origin of Murphy's Law. In a bid to explain this law in a simpler way, it was stated that if there was a wrong way of how or do something then someone would most definitely do it. This means that if there are many ways to lead to a destination, then one of those ways would lead to a disaster. If there is a possibility that something can go wrong, then it most definitely will.

In a bid to draw relevance to the scientific quotient of Murphy's Law, we find that it draws sense to the possibilities to a particular outcome. This means that there is the probability of various outcomes ensuing. When you take a look at its engineering explanation, you find that no matter how best a machine is efficient, it will in one way or another, breakdown at some point. With relation to logic, you will find that there are various shifts in your life which bring about balance. An absence of this will see to it that you live your life in a plateau-like manner, which brings about monotony. There are various instances in life that we are not proud to look back at. These are the instances that we have brought about shame and turmoil tom us. There is also a set of events that, when relating to, we find a sense of belonging because these are the moments when we were at our best. The implication of this law is that we should anticipate these bad times because once there is a possibility of something bad happening, then it most definitely will occur.

Most of the individuals who draw relevance to Murphy's Law are of the mindset that things will not go well, and in most cases, if they do go in the manner that they desire, they are less appreciative because they had an already formed perception that things would not go straight. When thin gas goes in the opposite manner, then they start to look for reasons why they did not succeed in whatever they were doing. The relevance of this law is premised on our various abilities to either succeed or fail in something. This law taps into this balance. In most instances, you will find that this law operates in our subconscious.

The idea that we cannot control our own fate is what sits at the helm of this particular law. This is known as fatalism. Fatalism is premised to the fact that you have no control whatsoever over things which are going on in your life. Take, for instance, we wake up each day with the intention of going through the day. We have no pre-determined control of what will happen throughout the day. Murphy's Law is also supported by a law known as the law of entropy. This is what is known as the natural law of things. It is to the effect that things would proceed in the manner that seems right. Most scholars have related this law as to the explanation of when people are in a difficult situation. The world of technology has drawn basis to this particular law as they are reminded time and again that systems will not function forever, and thus, there reaches a time when they will fail.

Occam's Razor

This is a principle which is to the effect that if there exist two explanations towards an outcome. With this type of principle, the one which often has the least number of assumptions is the one which in most cases, tends to work. In a bid to further explain this principle, you find that the more likely you are able to make more assumptions about a particular thing, the less likely you are able to arrive at a decision. The roots of this type of principle have been linked to one individual known as William Ockham. This individual studied logic and came up with this particular type of principle. When we are referring to this principle in Latin, it is known as Lex Persimoniae. Other people have also referred to it as the law of briefness. This particular law is of the impact that if you need to be exact in a manner that you do not generalize most issues. In a more direct manner, we can say that more things should not be used than are necessary.

In life, there are several explanations as to different outcomes; this means that there is a possibility that something might have taken place in a number of ways, although the explanation that is more exact is what is always close to the veracity of the events. If there is a complex explanation that surpasses a simpler one, then it of key importance that the complex one is put into consideration. This particular type of principle attempts to give explanations and not focus on the various entities that are available. This principle has the effect of attempting to draw an explanation to a particular phenomenon in a manner that is easy to decode. In a bid to further give an elaboration to this particular type of principle, we take a look at an instance;

Take this scenario whereby you wake up in the morning, and you find out that you have no fence. We can draw two explanations for this particular phenomenon. One is that the fence might have been washed away by the heavy rains the previous night, or it might have been a falling aircraft that has taken away the fence. Both these outcomes are relevant in that they are bound to occur in one way or another. The latter one, however, has to be preceded by a series of events in order to occasion its occurrence. The rarity of the latter event is what brings about its disqualification. The series of events that have to occur before you find the outcome of the latter event is what substantiates the last one as being possibly wrong. This principle works in the sense that by the fact that there is a simple explanation that can be given to the phenomena without beating about the bush, then perhaps this is the right answer.

There are other instances where the complex meaning that can be drawn to something is often one of the most correct. This means that an individual who is in evaluation needs to take into account a number of factors. You might use this scenario whereby you are on a raised ground, and in your hand is a piece of paper. The main aim of this exercise is to determine the amount of time that the paper will take in order to touch the ground. In mind, you ought to put into consideration the various factors that act as inhibiting factors, which will lead to an increase in the amount of time in which the paper takes to hit the floor. When you take into account air resistance, you are increasing the complexity of the issue. Thus in a bid to employ this principle, you can do away with the presence of air pressure. In a factual sense, this is not a correct explanation as to the time in which the paper takes to hit the ground as air resistance is a factor when it comes to calculating the amount of time taken by the piece of paper to fall. In a bid to give an accurate duration, the complex explanation is the one which, if adopted, will lead to a concrete assumption.

In the field of medicine, this type of principle has seen itself grow. This is to the effect whereby the simplest explanation is the one that goes rather than reflecting on a more complex ground. Take for instance there is a kid who has a wheeze in breathing. This kid would be more likely to be diagnosed with a simple whooping cough rather than relating this event to a birth effect, say Asthma. It is most important for the symptoms to be thought of as of in the simplest form. This is because you need not be administering a drug that has an overwhelming effect. The world of physics has employed the use of this principle in that it is to the effect that for every fiction to effect, there has to be the application of minimum energy. When it comes to theology, this particular principle has been given relevance as it tends to bring about the application of the bible in the simplest way possible. This means that individuals ought to stay devoid of the various contradictions to the literal sense of the bible and would rather adopt it as it is.

When it comes to correctional facilities, you find that the convicts who have committed a crime are more likely given a minimum sentence, not unless the gravity of the case has exceeded its limits. In relation to crimes, there are penal provisions that deal with those who have failed to honor the contract of co-existence between the government and the people. These provisions are normally written in a specific form that applies to a specific punishment. The criminal system in administering such punishment, do it in a manner that is of the least collator as possible. This is a shift from excessive penal practices that were present in the past.

Hanlon's Razor

As human beings, there is an equilibrium that ought to be achieved. Owing to this fact, our lives are characterized by various events ranging from good to bad. When good things happen to us, we are overwhelmed to the extent that we do not realize these moments. When something in the adverse takes place, we are forced to believe that there was a plot behind such occurrence taking place. Take, for instance, an individual who fails to hand in your assignment in time due to late minute rush. The thoughts that might be running through your mind is that this particular individual is inclined to the direction of you not succeeding. The basic answer that lies behind these explanations is simple to the extent that you would wish not to associate your ill thoughts to those accounts.

Hanlon's razor is a type of principle that can be elaborated in many ways. The easiest form in which one can explain this saying is that you should never draw the explanations of a particular phenomenon in the direction of malice or malevolency to events that have a source from normal stupidity. This type of principle is of key importance when eliminating possible sources to particular behaviors in the human. Nature. This type of principle is one which was influenced by Occam's razor. The principle has been relevant to most people to date.

In a bid to summarize this particular principle, one can deduce that you should never draw reference to malice to the things which can be easily given an explanation to by human behavior. This means that neglect should never be ignored in the face of thinking about the various ill outcomes. With this type of principle in our day to day life, we find that we are able to indulge in more meaningful relationships with other people. This way when people wrong us, we are in a position to give them room for empathy instead of shunning them away at the first instance. Many people have the tendency to dislike others just after the first strike. By the use of this principle, you find that you are in a position to give people second chances because you are of the view that everyone is human and is bound to make mistakes one way or another.

In our day to day ventures, we find that most of us tend to communicate with others and from this interaction, we have to make choices that impact our lives directly. This is what brings about the complexity in life. You will find that you are in a position where things are not working for you, and you are falling into mistakes time and again. When this happens, we would not want to carry the blame ourselves but rather to pin it on someone else. This is often the person who is next to us. This is because of the thought that they might have malicious intent. When it comes to throwing responsibilities to others, people will be quick to judge and even commit. When you are in the vicinity of another person messing up, we tend to forget about the numerous times that we have messed up. The problem that lies with human beings is that we tend to forget the numerous times that we have done wrong to someone else and focus on the presiding wrongs that others have done to us.

When you tend to assume that there was an ill intent behind the occurrence of an event, you find that you tend to worsen the situation. This is because you find that none of us has control over what others wanted to do. Most individuals who are smart in other facets of life have been found to be bound to making numerous mistakes. This is because mistakes are a general thing that does not happen by the inherent nature of a person but the natural order of things. When we are on the verge of getting overwhelmed with emotions, it is important to take into account the fact that we are bound to behave in that manner whenever we are frustrated. Once we are able to appreciate this fact, we are in a position to react positively towards these situations. Instances that make us become angry and agitated are most often the ones that are most valuable to us.

The best way of dealing with individuals who often bring us stress and turmoil is by extending simple education to them. This is to show them that you are a bigger person than them, and by that, you ensure that the same problem will not recur. The media has been one of the stakeholders that play a crucial role when it comes to this particular fact. You would find that the media dwells on various stories that have been characterized by an outrage of an individual that was merely misguided by ignorance or incompetence. With the developments in the media, we are getting to unearth those instances that have been accompanied by malice. Any content that has with it content suggesting malice has been seen to be unearthed.

When it comes to relationships, you find that this particular principle applies in a way that is crucial. The major problem that arises from various relationships is the feeling that the other party has become toxic. In this sense, you will see that the other party is the cause of all your problems. Once this has been established, you will start to deduce methods in which we can leave the relationship because it seems toxic to you. Many people who have been in relationships will tell you that letting the inner feeling malice intent accumulate will lead to the relationship eventually breaking. This type of principle has been seen with individuals who are experiencing a semantic barrier. Often this type of individual would be drawn towards the intention of not decoding what they are saying. This type of law is to the effect that it might not be in their best interests to seclude you.

The Principal of Pareto

The principal of Pareto is one that has also been known as the eighty twenty principal. Some people have time and again referred to this principle as that of the vital few. This has also been referred to as the rule of the factor sparsely. The principle plays with causes and effects and further states that in every instance whereby there is an eighty percent effect, you find that there are causes which are in twenty percent. This means that most of the outcomes of particular circumstances come from twenty percent of the causes. This principle was named after an Italian by the name Vilfredo Pareto. This is an individual who is said to have discovered this kind of principle while he was still at the university level. The first impact of this principle was related to the business world, whereby it was held that a percentage of eighty on the sales is dependent on the percentage of twenty of the clients.

When it comes to the field of mathematics, this type of principle has been encompassed in the power distribution, or as it is famously known as the Pareto distribution. This distribution accrues to specific parameters, and the naturally exhibit such attributes. When we draw our radar towards the world of economics, we find that Pareto was able to relate Italy's wealth in an Eighty twenty perspective. This way, he brought to relevance that a total of eighty percent e is often of Italy is owned by twenty percent of the population. In relation to other countries, the same curve ensued. When we look at the global income, we find that the way it is distributed, it is done so in an uneven manner that most of the wealth goes to a smaller group of individuals.

In the world of sports, this particular principle has showcased itself in the manner that there are simply fewer sporting activities. These particular activities have an eighty percent impact on your body and training. When an athlete is on the verge of training, we find that they are in a position to participate in varied activities. This being said and done, the athlete is mostly obliged to participate in varied training in order to affect fitness. The outcome is often tremendous, but the input was these simple exercises and routines. When you come to the world of occupational health, you find that most of the hazards are often minimal, say twenty percent. It is these particular hazards that see to it that there is an effect of eighty percent of the injuries. The principal sees to it that major hazards are minimalized. It not only achieves this through addressing hazards in an economical manner but also devising various techniques that would see to it a hazard that never happens again. Another field where the Pareto principle has set its roots is in the field of betting. With betting, you find that your stake was twenty percent, but your earnings are forthwith.

Sturge

The sturge rule is a particular type of rule that works in a bid to determine the desired number of groups when it comes to distribution and observation. This should be put into classes. The sturge rule has been an important aspect when it comes to settling on a particular type of bar. The sturge rule helps individuals to effectively represent information through the use of a histogram. With the sturge rule, data is represented in a manner that suggests tare put into that they are put into classes putting in mind the consideration of observation.

When data is represented in the manner which surpasses its normality, then more classes ought to be added. A number of sources have criticized the formation of Sturges in that they suggest the inclusion of scenes. Skewness was proposed by an individual known as Doane. The result of the introduction of skewness is that it results in histograms that are over-smooth. This is of crucial importance when it comes to drawing of the large histograms. When Doane's reason was implemented, then came the Sturge and Doanne's rule, which is of the effect that an individual will be able to maximize on the smoothness of the histogram. Although this proves that efficiency has been heightened, Sturge's rule has been recognized by various scholars, not drawing much effect on Doanne.

The problem that lies with this particular school of thought is the idea that they could have employed multiple binomial co-efficient, but the result of this would still be the same. This means that any number of classes would be achieved dependent on the multiple that has been used. The factor that has been outstanding for this particular type of principle is that it has been able to stand the taste of time because of the moderate (n), which is less than 200. The major problem with this type of rule is that the way it does its derivation is in a manner that is not correct. This rule fails to observe its place in statistics, and owing to this fact, you find that it defeats logic.

The formula of the Sturge's rule is to the effect that it considers histograms to ask bins. This is where the number values and data are recorded. In order to reach a total, one needs to make a summation of all the values that are in the bin. In order to arrive at the binomial expansion, one needs to replace q with (1-p). When this is achieved, and you are now solving k, you have then arrived at the Sturge's formula. With the formula at hand, it is considered in order to take the nearest integer. When we talk about implicit in this particular formula, we are referring to the mere assumption that there is a data that has been distributed normally and thus represented by a binomial coefficient of 0.5.

The Parkison's Laws On's Law

This type of principle is of the effect that works increases in volume in order to cover the amount of time that is needed for completion. The application of this particular type of law can be seen when it comes to organizational bureaucracy. This type of principle is one that came to be as a result of the thought process by an individual known as Cyril Parkinson. The principal has been appreciated by various scholars and has been used as an input in the current situation as a formula. Inclusion of crucial facts

The formula that exists to date is one that affects the explanation of how bureaucracies tend to build and establish themselves over time. The popularity of this particular type of law was one that was grave enough to see to it that it was translated into various languages. An example is the Soviet Union who used this particular type of principle after translating it. With the use of these factors, it becomes easier to explain the law. For instance, you have a task that you can complete in an hours' time. This task has been given to you with a deadline of one week. Relating this phenomenon to the principle at hand works in a bid to show that when you relate that amount of work to the time at hand, you will find that the work will have to expand in order to fit the available time. When we take a psychological look towards these particular aspects, we find that when you have a task and the time is just overwhelming; you will tend to be drawn towards restlessness and tension throughout the week where you could have achieved completion in relatively less than an hour.

With a grasp of this, we see that playing about these factors is what makes people look at various things in a discrepant manner. The lesson we can draw from such a conclusion is that we ought to accord work the right and enough amount of time in order to see to it that you do not waste too much of your time on the things that have less relevance. For instance, from the above scenario, if the individual would have completed the work in an hours' time, then the rest of the week would have been put too much resourceful use. There exists no indication whatsoever on the possibilities of an individual assigning particular and specific time towards a given task. What lies in between the lanes is that as human beings, we have the tendency to allocate more time to various tasks, and as a result, we tend to lose out majorly. This is because we spend so much time contemplating on various factors that we would have brushed through. The notion behind this principle is not to accomplish the work in a rush manner but rather to accomplish the task in a desirable manner.

Chapter 6: Intellectual Honesty

Intellectual honesty is a method of problem-solving in which truth is paramount. The ideas and attitudes given are not biased and are based on facts and honest responses. When this method is used, a person's believes and personal stands are not considered.

On the other hand, political affiliations and beliefs are not put into consideration. This is done in a manner in which the facts collected are only used in a truthful way with an aim to make sure that the decisions made are factual. Personal decisions are set aside, and honest responses are expected to be used. Intellectual honesty enables one to make decisions about a person or certain situations without being driven by his attitude, feeling, belief, or political opinion.

It is important for everyone to ensure that they are honest in everything they do. This is because an honest person is said to have some integrity, which lacks in so many people. When one knows the truth about something, and he or she actually states it, it means that they are intellectually honest.

When you are able to have very high standards when it comes to telling the truth, you will be considered to be intellectually honest. Being intellectually honest is not just about not lying; it is about being truthful even when you know that the truth will hurt many people. You will tell the whole truth without leaving anything out.

Intellectual honesty is mostly used when one is solving problems. It is, therefore, important to ensure that one is truthful enough to solve them without causing any conflicts among the given parties. With intellectual honesty, one has to ensure that they are unbiased as well as having an honest attitude. This skill can be demonstrated depending on the faith of the people around you, their beliefs, and also their political believes. This means that as much as intellectual honesty is used on people, it should never interfere with what they believe.

You cannot achieve intellectual honesty when you are not honest from within. You would be required to work on yourself before you can help those with honesty issues. This means that before you become a model, you have your honesty issues in check. There are people who are very observant and cannot open up to you unless you are honest enough to be trusted. This is why there is a need for you to ensure that you practice intellectual honesty before approaching them.

With intellectual honesty, you should be very firm about what you say. You should not allow people's opinions about your ideas to make you change what you said. You should ensure that you are principled in order for you to be able to stand for the truth. Someone who is intellectually honest does not care about what the people around them say as long as they are truthful.

Intellectual honesty is really important especially for people who are interactive. They could be socially or politically interactive. However, people have cultivated a culture of dishonesty, whereby they use it for their selfish gain. However, many people have learned the importance of being intellectually honest, and most of them have decided to follow that path. They are determined to eliminate the element of dishonesty when interacting with people.

It is with this mindset that many people have been able to get rid of intellectual dishonesty and replaced it with intellectual honesty. With intellectual honesty, one is able to relate well with the people around them. They may disagree with those who are rigid when it comes to change, but they will be able to auger well with all those who practice intellectual honesty.

One should also make sure that they do not omit facts related to something even as they apply honesty when solving issues. Someone should never interfere with the facts in order for them to get the favorable results they expect. There are those who are intellectually honest while there are those that are intellectually dishonest. It is, therefore, a good thing when one decides to be intellectually honest. For people without it, they should be able to nurture it. They will be required to ensure that they work on having the best values in order for them to be able to become honest intellectually.

With intellectual honesty, one is required to ensure that they are very open as well as honest when dealing with people. They need to be truthful by all means. One will be considered truthful when they are honest in everything they do.

Benefits of Intellectual Honesty

Intellectual honesty is of great importance to the human being as this helps in ensuring sanity and smooth transition ideas acquired in different aspects of life. Everyone wants to hang around an intellectually, honest person. There are many benefits that come with being Intellectual honest. I have discussed several below.

Enable one to be able to stick to Decisions: The first benefit is that intellectual honesty helps an individual in sticking to his decisions and principals in life. They do not keep changing what they said before to suit the people listening to them. One is able to have confidence in what he knows as truth and is not swayed by another phenomenon that surrounds him. When they speak the truth, nothing shakes them. They stick to the truth to the end. When a person observes intellectual honesty, he is able to make decisions based on truth and not being directed by other people.

Nurture Respect for Other People: Intellectual honesty helps a person in respecting other people's opinions. As we all know, it is always very important to respect those who are around us and especially respecting what they say or believe in. An intellectually honest person is always that person that will be able to admit that he is not all-knowing, and this will help him respect even those that are ahead of him in knowledge. They have the humility to accept their mistakes and correcting them before they result in conflicts.

Promote Reasonable Arguments: Intellectual honesty is essential in promoting reasonable arguments even in times when one in public. It helps one to be able to go argue with others in very mature ways considering that one needs not to defend his point in public without enough facts. They have to think through everything that comes out of their mouths before speaking. They are also accountable for the mistakes they make. Therefore we can say that intellectual honesty is evident when one is able to publicly express himself without considering or defending his opinions but rather being able to argue with facts. An intellectually honest person is not interested in winning an argument. Their goal is to ensure that they are truthful in everything they do or say whether they win the argument or not.

Accepting when Wrong: when one is Intellectually honesty, he is able to accept when he is wrong, intellectual honesty helps one to know when he is wrong, and instead of defending himself and justifying himself for being wrong, one is able to accept and move with facts. This greatly helps one to accept the facts and be able to be corrected in the right direction.it, therefore, plays a big part in ensuring that there is positive growth when it comes to our daily life. When one is able to be changed and is able to grow with facts, this promotes critical thinking in his life. In conclusion, we can say that for one to grow and be able to be respected and respect others, intellectual honesty is significant, and therefore, it should be cultivated and developed by all human beings.

Promotion of Authenticity: It is through honesty that one person around you will be able to know how you think and also how you feel. Many people would love to relate with someone who is honest since they know that they will be will get the truth about different things from you. You will be able to cultivate honesty among the people around you when you are honest hence the need to ensure that you are honest.

No Instances of Corruption: When people are intellectually honest, they will not accept anything related to corruption. This means that they will only deal with people who follow the right channels. It will, therefore, be easy to work with them since they have a sense of duty in themselves. They can, therefore, never allow any corrupt person around them.

Promotes Productivity: When one is intellectually honest, they tend to be dedicated to their work. They, therefore, ensure that all the tasks assigned to them are completed on time. This is of great help in ensuring that there is increased productivity. With increased productivity, businesses are able to grow, which in return enhances the economic stability as well as the development of a country. People who are intellectually intelligent make sure that they give their best when they are at their workplace. When they do this, they are also able to influence the people around them to become honest. This makes everyone an intellectually honest person, which makes it easy for them to deal with each other peacefully.

The building of Strong Relationships: You can never go wrong with intellectual honesty, especially when you would want to build healthy and strong relationships. The relationships will be built out of trust for each other. This makes everyone work harder in ensuring that they keep the trust between them. This helps them to be able to live in an environment that is friendly to everyone since they are all trustworthy. It makes it easy for them to interact and associate well with each other.

Things that Hinder one from being Intellectually Honest

Lack of values: In today's life, you will realize that we have a gap in intellectual honesty. This has been facilitated by a number of things that play a very big role in undermining intellectual honesty. A community that has its people lacking this essential value in life is in big danger because people are not able to make decisions based on facts but base on their believes, attitudes, and also their feelings at the time they are making such decisions. Some of the many things that hinder one from being intellectually honest are as discussed below.

Peer Association: It is important to note that peers and the power of association are one thing that has played a role in undermining and making people not to have intellectual honesty. Many people have ended up making decisions that are not based on facts out of fear of being de associated with peers or certain groups that they associate themselves in. This then makes them end up making decisions to please their peers because they fear that after making decisions that will not suit them, they may end up being put aside.

Personal Interests: Intellectual honesty has been hindered by personal interest. Many people will give information based on their personal gain as one will be able to consider the consequences of the decisions that he makes, either to his life or to his properties. Intellectual dishonesty, therefore, crops up where many people are not able to stand to factual decisions in life for they fear to lose in life.

Fear of losing peoples Support: In politics, for example, politicians are not able to withhold intellectual honesty because they have a fear of losing support from their followers. The world today has become a world where people don't like listening to facts, but rather they are swayed by lies thus, this is another thing that has made many people be intellectually dishonest.

Fear of Losing: Intellectual honesty has been brought about by fear of loss. Many people become intellectually dishonest and end up giving dishonest information because they fear to lose. Sometimes when one is honest, he may tend to be seen as an intellectual person or one that doesn't have any know-how of life matters. Through people knowing that you know, they tend to give you some respect; therefore, many people are dishonest because they fear to lose respect. In addition, sometimes, when one is truthful, he might lose properties.

Fear of Facing the Consequences: It is said that dishonesty comes from within us. It will normally happen to us when we have had difficult experiences that we have not been able to reconcile with. We will be dishonest when we are not sure about how the truth about different things may make us feel. We will, therefore, keep the truth to ourselves, hoping to be at peace with ourselves and the people around us. People will mostly prefer to remain dishonest to themselves instead of facing the painful truth.

For Protection: People may avoid being truthful in order for them to protect themselves from dishonest people. They will only give their trust to people who are truthful. They may have trusted the wrong people in the past hence the fear. They have to be sure enough before they can engage someone.

Intellectual Dishonesty

There is another breed of people who cannot be honest. They do not apply any standard when it comes to telling the truth. They do not see anything wrong with lying because they do not believe in honesty in the first place. When you hear that someone is intellectually dishonest, just know that they are doing it deliberately. It is not something that one is born with. However, one may be intellectually dishonest without knowing it. For example, when you are lying to yourself, you may not realize that you are intellectually dishonest.

Intellectual dishonesty is considered to interfere with honesty. One cannot be dishonest and expect the people around them to be honest with them. People around you will decide whether to be honest with you or not, depending on whether you are honest yourself or not. When they realize that you are intellectually honest with them, they will open up to you in a truthful manner. It is, therefore, important to ensure that you are truthful in order for people around you to be honest with you too.

Disadvantages of Intellectual Dishonesty

Intellectual dishonesty is a situation when one is not able to give the truth about circumstances. We find that in the current world, many people are not able to give factual information and therefore end up making decisions to fit their beliefs, attitudes, and political opinions. This has made people be intellectually dishonest. As we can see, intellectual dishonest has many disadvantages in our life. Some of these disadvantages are;

Leads to Disagreements – intellectual dishonesty has led to many disagreements. This has been because people make decisions and also give information that will favor them rather than basing their decisions and arguments on facts. When every person in the argument tends to defend his points even when they are wrong, this will at the end of it sprout into arguments and disagreements as everyone will tend to think that they are right and the other party is wrong.

Poor upbringing – intellectual dishonesty among people in the current generation has led to many children getting wrong examples of characters from them. This leads to the children growing and emulating the seniors; thus, they grow up being intellectually dishonest.

Corruption- corruption of both the mind and in the aspect of properties has been necessitated by having a generation that is not intellectually honest. This is because people have learned to use lies for personal gains. This results in a crooked generation.

Marital conflicts – intellectual dishonesty has made many families be engaged in conflicts and, furthermore, even leading to breakups. When the wrong information is given to your partners, trust tends to be eroded in the relationship and end up breakups.

More Corruption: This is because people have no values. They do not see the need to be truthful since they are used to a culture of dishonesty. An intellectually dishonest person may not have value for the people around them. This is because they do not see the need to relate well with them. The world and the people in it, therefore, end up being full of corrupt people.

Stress: Most people will end up being stressed. They cannot open up to the people around them and even their business partners. They will be in fear so they cannot open up to the people around them. This makes people not to open up since the people around them are not honest with them

Selfishness: All they care about is what they get from the people or businesses. They do not care about people's feelings even when they wrong them. There is no time when they will team up with the people around them to make things better for them. Such people also do not take responsibilities seriously. Their aim is only to exploit the people around them. This makes it so difficult to work with them since you cannot agree on anything with them, and also, they cannot be trusted.

As we can see from above, intellectual honesty should be embraced by all for a better life and also in order to have a generation that will be of importance to society. We always strive to make sure that there is honest communication between the people around us. We are therefore supposed to ensure that we identify the things that may be making the people around dishonest in order for us to eliminate them.

Whenever you find people dishonest, there must be things that may have made them choose to keep the truth from you. If the issue is not identified, they might never open up to you in an honest way. It is, therefore, everyone's responsibility to ensure that they develop trust between them and the recipients in order for them to be able to ensure that they become honest among themselves. You can form trust by ensuring that you accept criticism as well as new ideas from them without undermining them. Once you do that, you will be able to be honest with them also without making them feel offended about it.